ROPE TECHNIQUES
IN MOUNTAINEERING

ROPE TECHNIQUES
IN MOUNTAINEERING

INCORPORATING IMPROVISED TECHNIQUES
IN MOUNTAIN RESCUE

BILL MARCH

CICERONE PRESS
POLICE SQUARE, MILNTHORPE

First published as Modern Rope Techniques 1973
2nd Edition Revised 1976
Reprinted 1977, 1978, 1980
Reprinted 1981 (Revised)
Reprinted 1983
3rd Edition Revised 1985
Reprinted 1986, 1988, 1990
Reissued as Rope Techniques 1992
Reprinted 1994, 1997

ISBN 1 85284 120 6

Cicerone Press
2 Police Square
Milnthorpe
Cumbria
England

Front Cover:
Central Pillar, Esk Buttress, Lake District.
Climbers: Louise Dickie, Mark Glaister.
Photo by Bill Birkett

CONTENTS

INTRODUCTION
Modern Rope Techniques in Mountaineering

Since its inception in 1973 the context and format of this book has been revised twice and yet the pace of development of mountaineering techniques has continued at an ever increasing rate. The work of the U.I.A.A. has added considerably to our knowledge of belaying and there have been many improvements in materials and design of mountaineering equipment. This third revision has presented me with the considerable problem of limiting the scope of the book and of necessity I have had to limit the amount of material. This book is not a comprehensive instructional manual which would run into many hundreds of pages to cover all aspects of modern techniques. It is rather a handbook for the experienced climber who wishes to broaden his knowledge of techniques, in particular those associated with improvised rescue. I have not, therefore, dealt with the many different kinds of harnesses on the market but have assumed their operational efficiency. Where the techniques described are complex I have attempted to break down the diagrams into 'annotated sequences' to facilitate understanding. It is strongly suggested that these step by step instructions be closely followed. It is also very important to practice the technique illustrated in a controlled situation when all the normal mistakes can be made in safety. It will be found that such factors as the length of sling and position of karabiners are critical and these should be determined by careful practice under controlled conditions, i.e. back-up systems and stand by helpers.

In conclusion it should be remembered that there is no substitute for practical experience in developing and acquiring mountaineering skill. The key factor in the mountaineering equation is judgement - only the individual can make the final decision on what anchor to select and/or place, what technique to use, and what safety procedures to follow. This book is only an aid to assist you in the attainment of the practical aspects of this goal. At the end of the book you will find 'The Essential Rescue Techniques' which I have written to give you an operational framework of reference to assist you in the learning journey.

Safe Climbing,
Bill March.

CHAPTER I
ROPES, KNOTS, HARNESSES AND TRAGSITZ

The rope is the primary equipment carried by the mountaineer and is used for belaying, hoisting, lowering, rappelling and transportation (stretchers and improvised carries). The first climbing ropes were made of natural fibre, e.g. Italian hemp and manila. Natural fibre ropes were not very strong in relation to size, had limited shock absorbing properties, were prone to rotting and mildew, absorbed water and were stiff and unmanageable when frozen. After the Second World War nylon replaced hemp as the material for climbing rope construction for the following reasons:

(i)   Light and flexible.

(ii) High tensile stength because of continuous filaments used in its construction.

(iii) High shock absorption capacity due to its elasticity.

(iv) Resistent to rot and mildew.

(v)   Low water absorption.

As a material nylon does, however, suffer from the following disadvantages:

(i)   Deteriorates at 400°F and melts at 480°F. These figures may be different for new improved derivatives of nylon. *Avoid nylon running over static nylon to prevent friction melting.

(ii) Deteriorates on prolonged exposure to ultra violet light.

(iii) May be damaged by chemicals, oils and acids.

(iv) Is subject to chaffing by abrasion over rough surfaces and cutting of internal filaments by grit particles especially if a dirty rope is trodden on.

(v)   Cuts fairly easily on sharp surfaces - sharp rock edge, crampon spike, ice axe adze.

The climber may also use polypropylene ropes or nylon non-stretch ropes for fixed line where there is no shock loading. Neither of these ropes are suitable for lead climbing. It is essential that all climbing ropes can absorb the energy generated in a fall minimizing the possibility of injuring the climber. The Union International des Associations d'Alpinisme are an organization who have set standards for climbing ropes. No one should use a rope for climbing unless it has the U.I.A.A. stamp of approval. The U.I.A.A. standard fall test is an 80 kilogram load dropped 5 metres on a free fall. There are now multi fall ropes available exceeding the earlier U.I.A.A. requirements of 3 falls. Another development has been the introduction of water resistent treatments for ropes to reduce water absorption, however, these tend to wear off with use.

Rope Construction: The rope may be of two types of construction: hawser laid with three strands of nylon filaments twisted in a spiral, and kernmantel where fibres are arranged longitudinally in a core and covered with a braided sheath. Nowadays kernmantel rope has almost completely supplanted hawser-laid in general climbing usage. Hawser-laid ropes have the advantage that the three strands can be unravelled and joined together in an emergency thus increasing the length of the rope by three and of course decreasing its strength proportionately. When a hawser-laid rope twists or kinks this distortion can weaken the rope by 15%. Never try to pull out a kink since this will lead to a complete hackle which reduces the rope strength by one third. The kernmantel rope is less liable to kink than hawser-laid rope and is more resistant to abrasion and easier to handle. A new kernmantel rope initially may appear difficult to grip but as its surface abrades with use the 'gripability' improves. This surface fuzziness is from wear of the surface fibres and does not appreciably reduce the rope strength.

Size of Rope: The size and length of rope carried depends on the activity rope lengths, 120ft. (37 metres); 150ft. (45 metres); and 165ft. (50 metres). The middle length 150ft. appears to be the most popular in use at the present time. The rope diameter recommended for single rope climbing is 11mm (7/16) and for double rope climbing is 9mm (3/8). Smaller diameter ropes are available in diameters 8mm, 7mm, 6mm, and 5mm. These thinner ropes are used for slings and prusik loops, rappel slings.

Care of Rope: Climbing ropes should be well cared for to prevent damage during use - avoid sharp edges by careful rope management techniques. When the rope is dirty wash in luke warm water with a mild detergent to remove damaging grit. Store in a cool dark place and avoid stretching or placing near a direct heat source such as a stove. Check the rope for damage visually and by squeezing the core beneath the mantle. It is difficult to recommend an average life of a rope, however, if the mantle is damaged, the rope sustains a severe fall or the core is distorted then the rope should be retired.

ROPE CONSTRUCTION

HAWSER LAID

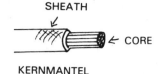

SHEATH

CORE

KERNMANTEL

KINK

IF A KINK EXTENDED
IT BECOMES A 'HOCKLE'
AND PERMANENT DAMAGE
IS CAUSED

LAP COILS ON BELAY (BUTTERFLY COILS)

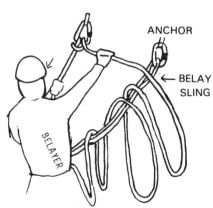

ANCHOR

← BELAY SLING

BELAYER

LAP COILS FROM A DIRECT BELAY
ON MUNTER HITCH AVOIDS DROPPING
ROPE ON SECOND
(SNOW AND ICE CLIMBING)

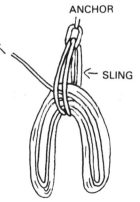

ANCHOR

← SLING

LAP COILS ON SLING FOR
PAYING OUT TO LEADER
USEFUL IF THERE ARE SNAGS
BELOW BELAY STANCE

COILING THE ROPE

Mountain Coil: The rope is coiled and the free ends are fastened by a single whipping of 6 turns. The two free ends may be further secured with a reef knot.

Butterfly Coil: The rope is laid in a double loop starting from the middle and the end is wrapped around and threaded through the eye as shown in the diagram and looped through itself.

Lap Coil: This type of coil is useful when on the belay and you do not wish the rope to fall below and impede the climber below, i.e. on a snow and ice pitch where it may be damaged by crampon spikes or ice axe pick. The rope is laid in a series of S loops hanging on either side of the climber's knee - it can be held loosely in a sling loop or hang over the belay anchor. This method is also useful when there is a danger of the loose loops of rope snagging or jamming in cracks below the belayer.

Knots: The knots which are used by the climber should have the following characteristics:

1. Easy to tie.
2. Strong and secure.
3. Easy to untie after having been under load.
4. Easy to check at a glance that the knot is tied correctly.

FOUR WAYS OF COILING THE ROPE

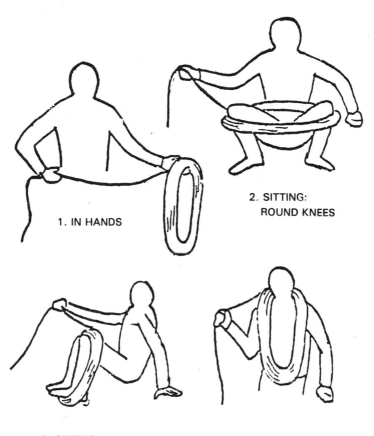

1. IN HANDS

2. SITTING:
   ROUND KNEES

3. SITTING:
   AROUND KNEES — FEET

4. OVER HEAD -
   AROUND NECK

CARRYING THE COIL

THE FIVE POPULAR METHODS OF CARRYING
THE ROPE ARE:

1. IN PACK

2. OVER HEAD -
UNDER ONE ARM

BACK

3. SPLIT COIL -
PUT ARMS THROUGH

4. ON BACK
WITH BOTH ARMS
THROUGH

5. ON BACK
WITH ENDS CROSSED
OVER CHEST

BASIC KNOTS

Figure of Eight on the Bight

This is tied on a loop of rope and used as the end tie in climbing. It is a strong knot adjusted by feeding one strand of the rope through the knot and tightening afterwards. Its great advantage is it is comparatively easy to tie and if tied wrongly, is still quite safe as an overhand knot, or as an expanded figure of 8. The end tail of rope should be tied off in a thumb knot around the main rope. A single Figure of Eight can be converted into a Figure of Eight on the Bight by threading the tail end back through the knot following the line of the original 8. When tying the Figure of Eight on the Bight, always ensure that the main rope lies on the outside of the first bend in the knot. (See point X in the diagram). If this is on the inside, the knot is weakened.

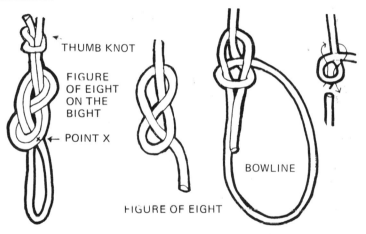

THUMB KNOT

FIGURE OF EIGHT ON THE BIGHT

← POINT X

FIGURE OF EIGHT

BOWLINE

Bowline

This is the old classic knot in climbing which is not as strong as the figure of eight knot but still in common use as a direct tie onto the rope. Easily adjusted by feeding through on one side of the knot. This knot is not always effective in kernmantel rope and should always be tied off with a thumb knot around the main rope.

Bowline on the Coil

This knot is used by American climbers and has the advantage of providing a cushioning effect on a waist tie because of the elasticity provided by the additional coils. It is simply a bowline tied around several coils of rope rather than one coil.

13

Fisherman Knot
Used for joining two ropes together. Can be tied single or double.

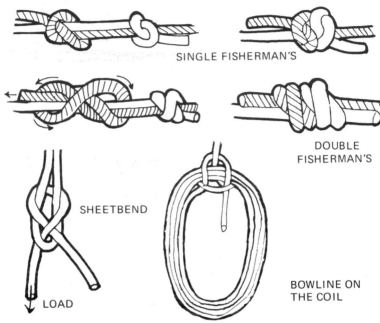

SINGLE FISHERMAN'S

DOUBLE FISHERMAN'S

SHEETBEND

LOAD

BOWLINE ON THE COIL

Sheet Bend
A useful knot used for joining rope of unequal thickness and for joining slings which need to be adjusted easily. May be tied single or double and also can be locked with a thumb knot.

TAPE KNOT

Tape Knot
The standard knot used for fastening tape slings. The tails of the knot should be secured by stitching or adhesive tape after the knot has been tightened for additional security.

Bowline on the Bight

This is simply a bowline tied on a bight of rope with the end loop passed over the half completed knot (see diagram). It gives an easily adjusted sit sling with two loops for the legs, or may be used as a shoulder harness with a loop crossed over each shoulder and under the opposite arm. The harness can be tightened by feeding one strand of rope through the knot.

Figure of Eight on the Bight with Two Loops

This is a single figure of eight knot tied on a bight of rope with the end loop passed over the completed knot. (see diagram). It is used in the same way as the Bowline on the bight.

ROPE SEATS

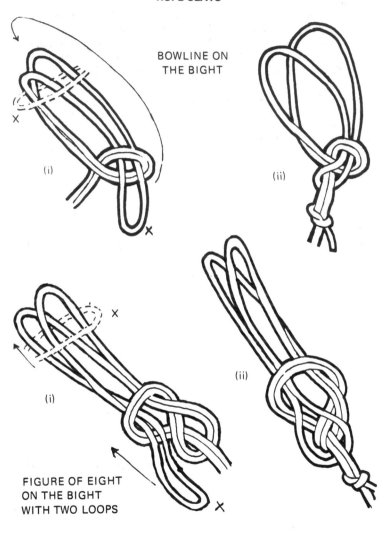

BOWLINE ON
THE BIGHT

(i)

(ii)

FIGURE OF EIGHT
ON THE BIGHT
WITH TWO LOOPS

(i)

(ii)

Triple Bowline

The triple bowline is a bowline tied in a bight of rope and gives three loops which can be worn as a sit sling, chest sling, or a full harness. All harnesses are tightened up by feeding one strand of rope right through the knot and the harness. This takes some time but it is essential that the harness is a secure fit on the body.

a. Sit sling - one loop around the chest and one for each leg.
b. Chest harness - one loop under the arm pits and around the chest, the other two crossed over the shoulder and under the arm pits.
c. Full harness - one loop for each leg and one diagonally across one shoulder and under the opposite arm pit. The harness is adjusted so that the knot is above the centre of gravity - just below the sternum. The loops at the back may all be clipped together with a karabiner or tied together with a sling to give greater security.

Thomson Knot

Another knot which provides a three loop harness and is more simple to tie than the triple bowline, is the 'Thomson Knot' (This was shown to me by Jack Thomson of Glenmore Lodge and has no specific name). The rope is looped to form an S with an extra loop and then 4 strands of rope are taken and tied in an overhand knot. This knot may be adjusted in the same way as the triple bowline by feeding one strand of rope through the knot and the harness.

Seat Harness from a Swami Belt

The Swami belt is 12ft. of 1″ nylon tape normally wrapped 3 or 4 times around the waistband and tied with a tape knot. It is widely used in the USA as a climbing harness. The swami belt can be used to make a sit harness when required. First take one turn around the waist and tie an overhand knot in front, pass the two ends between the legs and around the buttocks and tie each with an overhand knot into the sides of the existing waist tie. Next thread the ends through the front tapes of the original overhand and tie them together with a tape knot.

Sit Slings

Slings are a standard piece of equipment carried by climbers. Some should be of the required length to be used for making improvised sit slings and chest harnesses. One inch tape slings make very comfortable harnesses which are less cumbersome than the rope slings.

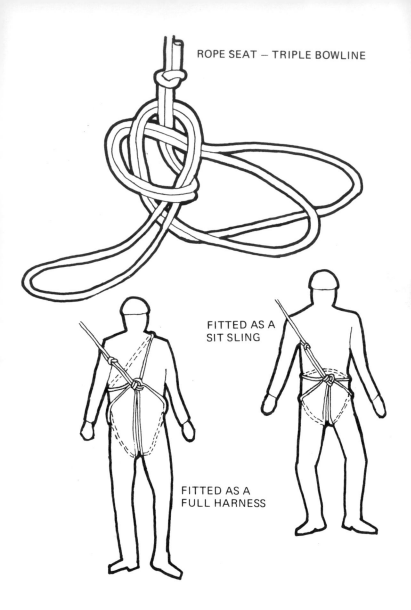

ROPE SEAT — TRIPLE BOWLINE

FITTED AS A
SIT SLING

FITTED AS A
FULL HARNESS

THOMSON KNOT

(i) MAKE A SERIES OF LOOPS   (ii) TIE AN OVERHAND KNOT

SEAT HARNESS FROM A SWAMI BELT

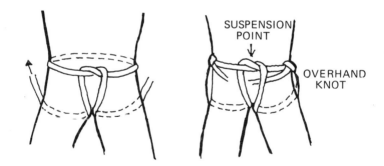

(i) TIE AN OVERHAND KNOT AND
PASS ENDS BETWEEN THE
LEGS AND AROUND BUTTOCKS

(ii) TIE ENDS INTO WAIST WITH
OVERHAND KNOTS AND
THREAD THROUGH FRONT
TAPE. TIE ENDS TOGETHER
WITH TAPE KNOT

Dulfer Seat

This is one of the most comfortable sling seats and is easily arranged. Take a sling and karabiner and pass around the back at waist level. Drop one loop of the sling weighted with a karabiner at the back and pull through the legs. Clip onto the two loops of the sling held in the front. This gives support to the waist and both legs. The karabiner can be clipped into the waistline to hold the seat up.

Double Sit Sling Seat

Step into double sling crossed at the front, drop on loop at the back and pull up between the legs to clip onto the front with a karabiner.

Figure of Eight Seat

Twist a sling to form a figure of eight and step into the two loops. Clip a karabiner at the cross over point and up into the waistline. If the sling is too long, tie off the surplus in an overhand knot to get the required tension.

Thigh Loop

A quick sit sling is a short loop around the thigh clipped into the waistline.

SIT SLINGS

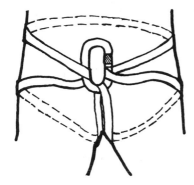

DULFER SEAT

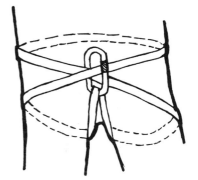

DOUBLED SIT SLING SEAT

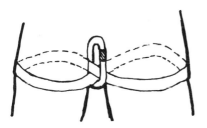

FIGURE OF EIGHT SEAT

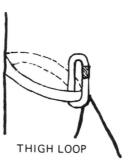

THIGH LOOP

CHEST HARNESSES

Parisian Baudrier

This harness may be made from a normal eight foot sling passed through one arm and taken around the back and under the other arm. The sling is tied off in the front with a sheet bend thus locking all the parts of the harness.

Crossed Sling Baudrier

This a requires a shorter sling and is made by looping the sling over the head and under the arm then twisting a second loop back over the head and under the other arm. It is not as effective as the Parisian Baudrier because it tends to ride up in the front when under load.

Improvised Chest Harness

A useful improvised chest harness may be tied using 5 metres of 7mm tensile cord. Wrap the cord around the chest 3 or 4 times and tie at the front with a bowline on the coil (p.27). Pass one length over the shoulder, thread through the back loops, twist over itself and bring to the front where it is tied to the other free end using a single fishermans knot.

Improvised Seat Harness

Take 5 metres of 7 or 9mm tensile rope, double and tie an overhand knot ½ an arm span from the looped end. Place the loop around the waist allowing the two free ends to drop between the legs. Thread the free ends through the front of the loops and tie in a reef knot across the lower abdomen. Thread the remaining rope through the loops once more, tie an overhand knot, and pass the free ends through the chest harness and tie back on itself to make a single fisherman's knot, see p.27(4) and p.28.

Full Harnesses

It is possible to construct a full harness using a combination of sit sling and chest harness. The Parisian Baudrier combined with the Dulfer seat makes a comfortable full harness. The Baudrier is tied with an extra long sling giving a long end loop which is clipped into the Dulfer seat, tensioned and tied off in an overhand knot at the suspension point. An adjustable harness can be made by attaching the rope directly to the Dulfer seat and fastening the chest harness to the rope with a prusik sling. (Fig. page 25). The prusik sling is tied to the chest harness loop with a sheet bend and is short enough to be easily reached by the climber. The prusik can be slid up and down the rope, thus adjusting the angle of the climber to the lower rope. This is the normal barrow boy rig in a stretcher lower.

Many other combinations are possible using different sit slings, knots, and chest harnesses. It is important to lock off the suspension point of the harness where it is attached to the rope to prevent movement.

CHEST HARNESSES

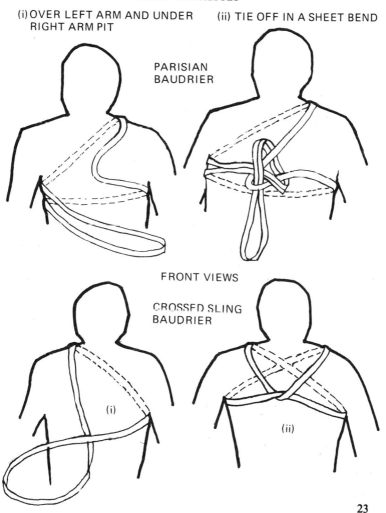

(i) OVER LEFT ARM AND UNDER RIGHT ARM PIT

(ii) TIE OFF IN A SHEET BEND

PARISIAN BAUDRIER

FRONT VIEWS

CROSSED SLING BAUDRIER

(i)

(ii)

IMPROVISED SEAT AND CHEST HARNESS
USING TAPE SLINGS

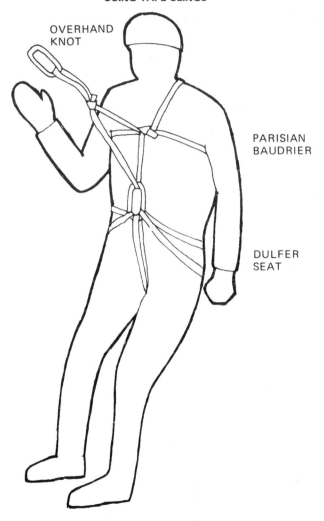

OVERHAND
KNOT

PARISIAN
BAUDRIER

DULFER
SEAT

AN ADJUSTABLE SEAT AND CHEST HARNESS
USING TAPE SLINGS AND A PRUSIK

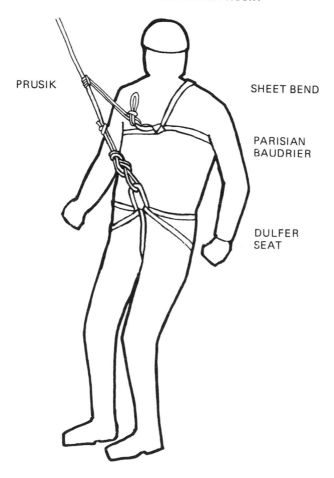

PRUSIK

SHEET BEND

PARISIAN
BAUDRIER

DULFER
SEAT

IMPROVISED CHEST HARNESS TIED WITH
5m TENSILE CORD, 7mm DIAMETER

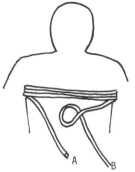

1) TUCK LOOP UNDER WRAPS.

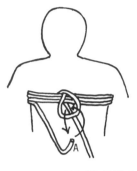

2) BOWLINE TIE ON THE COIL (i)

3) (ii)

4) (iii) PASS ROPE END B TO BACK

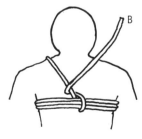

5) BACK VIEW, THREAD B THROUGH ITSELF AT BACK.

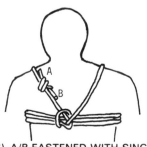

6) A/B FASTENED WITH SINGLE FISHERMAN'S KNOT AT FRONT.

IMPROVISED HARNESS FOR GLACIER TRAVEL
(USED WITH CHEST HARNESS)
5m OF 7-9mm TENSILE ROPE

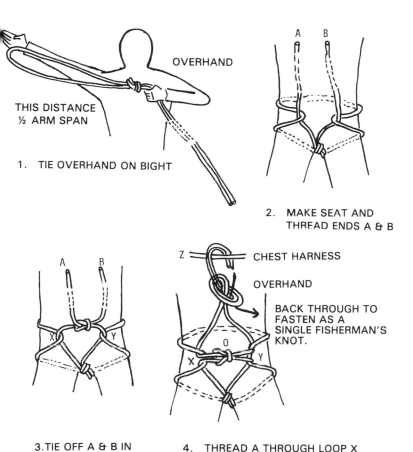

OVERHAND

THIS DISTANCE
½ ARM SPAN

1. TIE OVERHAND ON BIGHT

A   B

2. MAKE SEAT AND
   THREAD ENDS A & B

Z   CHEST HARNESS

OVERHAND

BACK THROUGH TO
FASTEN AS A
SINGLE FISHERMAN'S
KNOT.

3. TIE OFF A & B IN
   SQUARE KNOT (REEF)

4. THREAD A THROUGH LOOP X
   THREAD B THROUGH LOOP Y
   TIE IN OVERHAND O

5. LINK THROUGH CHEST HARNESS Z AND BACK THROUGH
   FIRST OVERHAND. THEN TIE OFF IN SECOND OVERHAND TO
   COMPLETE SINGLE FISHERMAN'S

27

IMPROVISED FULL BODY HARNESS

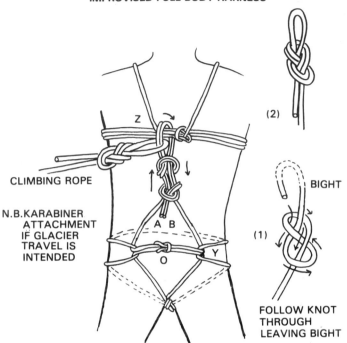

(2)

CLIMBING ROPE

N.B. KARABINER
ATTACHMENT
IF GLACIER
TRAVEL IS
INTENDED

BIGHT

(1)

FOLLOW KNOT
THROUGH
LEAVING BIGHT

LINK CORDS A B THROUGH CHEST HARNESS Z AFTER TYING IN OVERHAND. THREAD BACK THROUGH FIRST OVERHAND AND TIE OFF IN SECOND OVERHAND TO COMPLETE SINGLE FISHERMAN'S KNOT. TIGHTEN.

Improvised leg loops

Swami belts and climbing belts can be easily converted into comfortable sit harnesses by using 40-45mm. wide webbing. First take a length of tape 2.5 metres long and tie thigh loops using a tape knot. Adjust the thigh loops to fit comfortably and at the same time ensuring the connecting tape between them fits just below the waist belt under load. The rope can be tied through this connecting tape and the waist belt. It is necessary to attach the back of the thigh loop to the waist belt to prevent them slipping down. Another improvement is a separate stitched loop of tape joining the thigh loops and the waist belt at the front. In the interests of safety the climbing rope should always be tied through the connecting tape of the thigh loops and the waist belt.

Full Harness using a Sling

It is possible to make an emergency improvised harness using a standard length sling and a karabiner as shown in the diagram. The main disadvantage of this is the loading on the crotch of the climber.

CONVERTING WAISTBELT INTO SIT HARNESS

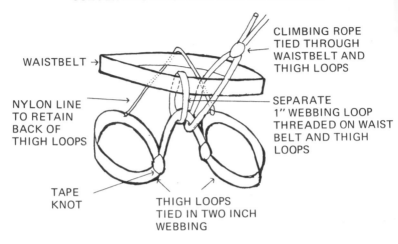

WAISTBELT →

CLIMBING ROPE
TIED THROUGH
WAISTBELT AND
THIGH LOOPS

NYLON LINE
TO RETAIN
BACK OF
THIGH LOOPS

SEPARATE
1" WEBBING LOOP
THREADED ON WAIST
BELT AND THIGH
LOOPS

TAPE
KNOT

THIGH LOOPS
TIED IN TWO INCH
WEBBING

IMPROVISED HARNESS FROM 1" TAPE SLING

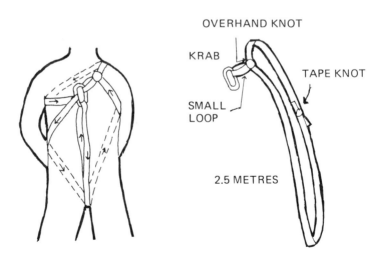

OVERHAND KNOT

KRAB

TAPE KNOT

SMALL
LOOP

2.5 METRES

Harnesses

At the present time there is a multitude of harnesses on the market and the Union International Association d'Alpinism are concerned with standardisation. It is important to note that the improvised harnesses do not fulfill the prsent UIAA requirements and the climber must be aware of the limitation of improvised harnesses. The basic requirements of a climbing harness are:

i.   The load of the falling climber should be taken on the strongest part of his body i.e. the thighs and to a certain extent on the ribs. Compression of the spine should be avoided.

ii. The harness should be attached to the rope above the centre of gravity of the climber ideally at the sternum where the ribs are joined. This ensures that an unconscious climber will be held in a sitting position.

iii. The harness should not restrict the breathing and circulation of the free hanging climber.

The acceptance of the above requirements infers that a full body harness is necessary i.e. chest/sit harness. This harness can be one part full body harness or two part consisting of separate chest harness and sit harness which can be combined or used separately depending on the situation. In the latter it should be possible to remove the sit harness in order to carry out necessary bodily functions without detaching oneself completely from the rope. To fulfil this function the climbing rope is used to fasten the chest and body harness together. The use of a karabiner is undesirable because of the risk of injury to the falling climber's face. One disadvantage of this system is that if the climber wishes to untie from the rope for any reason his chest harness is unfastened and depending on the design of his sit harness this may also be unfastened. It is desirable that both chest and sit harnesses be self fastening and this has led to the development of the one piece full harness which may restrict the carrying out of bodily functions. A compromise is to fasten the sit harness and chest harness together with a separate length of rope and fasten the climbing rope at the sternum. This is a one point suspension which is less comfortable than a correctly adjusted two point suspension. There are, therefore, pros and cons for different systems and the climber should be aware of these when using the different harnesses and different methods of attachment.

One and Two Point Attachment

The diagrams show the methods of attaching the rope at two suspension points using a fishermans knot or a bowline. It is very important to adjust the attachment so the climber is held in the correct sitting up position even when unconscious. The two point attachment is more comfortable and safer than the one point attachment as there is less danger of spinal compression. The best way to check the correct adjustment is to hang free in the harness.

METHODS OF ATTACHMENT TO HARNESS

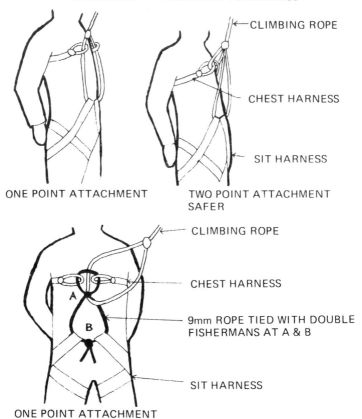

CLIMBING ROPE

CHEST HARNESS

SIT HARNESS

ONE POINT ATTACHMENT

TWO POINT ATTACHMENT SAFER

CLIMBING ROPE

CHEST HARNESS

9mm ROPE TIED WITH DOUBLE FISHERMANS AT A & B

SIT HARNESS

ONE POINT ATTACHMENT TO FULL HARNESS

32

KNOTS USED TO TWO POINT ATTACHMENT OF ROPE TO CHEST AND SIT HARNESS

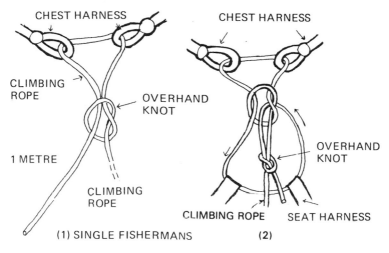

CHEST HARNESS

CHEST HARNESS

CLIMBING ROPE

OVERHAND KNOT

1 METRE

CLIMBING ROPE

(1) SINGLE FISHERMANS

OVERHAND KNOT

CLIMBING ROPE

SEAT HARNESS

(2)

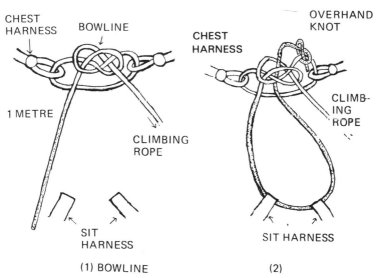

CHEST HARNESS

BOWLINE

CHEST HARNESS

OVERHAND KNOT

1 METRE

CLIMBING ROPE

CLIMB-ING ROPE

SIT HARNESS

(1) BOWLINE

SIT HARNESS

(2)

Improvised Tragsitz Using a Climbing Rope Only

It is possible to construct a tragsitz using only a climbing rope. First take a coil of rope and pay off three coils one side and four coils the other side. Next divide the remaining rope coils evenly into two and split the rope, tying the centre of the split rope coils with line. Take the one end of the three coils and tie a clove hitch on the bottom of one of the rope coils, take the rope across and tie off on the bottom of the other rope coil in the same way forming a loop. Next take the other end of four coils and tie a clove hitch at the top of the rope coil. Take the rope across in a long loop to the other rope coil and tie off in the same way. Now take the rope back in a short loop to the first coil and fasten in a clove hitch. Take the two long loops, one from the top and one from the bottom, and tie a figure of eight at the end of each. Place casualty in split ropes on carry man's back. The carry man sits astride the bottom ropes, and the casualty is held by the top ropes. The short loop is passed under the casualty's arms and across the chest or under his arms and over his head.

IMPROVISED TRAGSITZ USING A CLIMBING ROPE

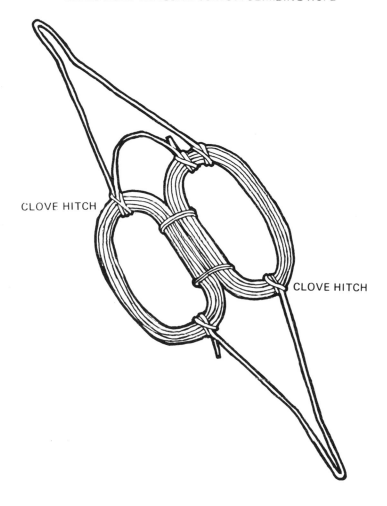

CLOVE HITCH

CLOVE HITCH

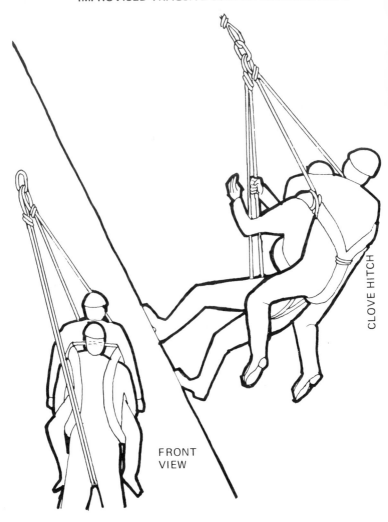

FRONT
VIEW

CLOVE HITCH

Tragsitz

The improvised tragsitz is a method of carrying an injured climber off the cliff on the back of the rescuer. There are many different methods and one is shown here as an example. First rig both casualty and carry man in full harnesses of Dulfer seats and Parisian baudriers. Attach the carry man to a prusik sling fastened a few feet up the rope. The casualty is carried in a split rope carry tied at the front of the carry man with a piece of line. The prusik sling is adjusted so that the weight of the casualty is taken on the load rope and the carry man provides the legs to keep him away from the rock face. A prusik loop can be attached to the rope for the carry man to hold onto for extra support.

Unless there is a high belay the start of the tragsitz lower exerts considerable strain on the carry man until all the forces are resolved. Once over the edge the carry is comparatively easy if the tragsitz has been correctly adjusted before starting.

Lowering the Tragsitz

1. By a climber above, through a karabiner brake.
2. By the carry man himself lowering through a karabiner brake anchored above.
3. By a counter weight system (p.39) with the carryman lowering himself and the casualty through a top pulley karabiner controlling the decent by using a friction brake attached to his harness.
4. Rappelling with the casualty and the carryman attached to a single suspension point which in turn is attached to a friction device. In this instance the doubled rappel rope could either be passed under the leg for greater friction/control or split in two and held apart, one in each hand.

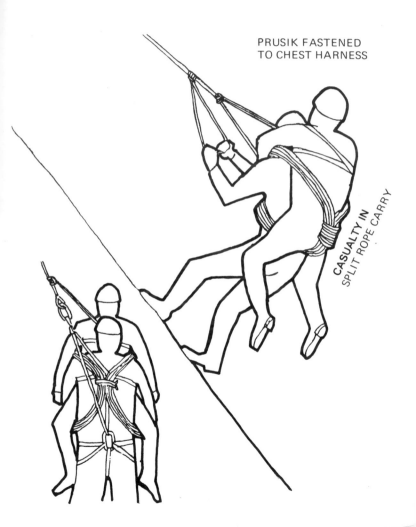

PRUSIK FASTENED
TO CHEST HARNESS

CASUALTY IN
SPLIT ROPE CARRY

COUNTER WEIGHT RESCUE
HALF ROPE LENGTH

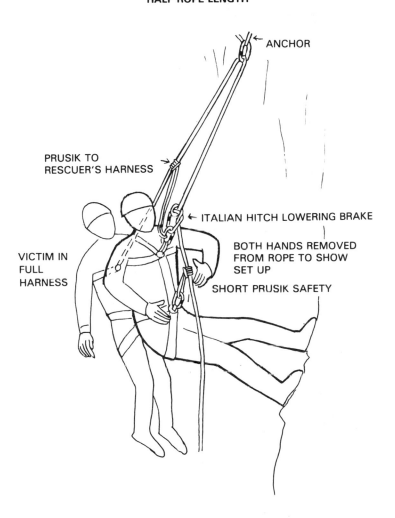

ANCHOR

PRUSIK TO
RESCUER'S HARNESS

ITALIAN HITCH LOWERING BRAKE

BOTH HANDS REMOVED
FROM ROPE TO SHOW
SET UP

VICTIM IN
FULL
HARNESS

SHORT PRUSIK SAFETY

CHAPTER II
BELAYING 1
WAIST BELAY/ITALIAN HITCH

One of the fundamental skills of the mountaineer which has seen considerable development over the past few years has been the practice of belaying. This chapter is an attempt to examine critically the present situation and evaluate the pros and cons of different methods. The experienced climber requires a repertoire of technical expertise and knowledge to draw upon: he needs to be conversant with different methods so that in the event of an emergency he can improvise with the minimum of equipment whatever the situation. For the purpose of this book belaying is defined as the safeguarding of one climber by another using the rope in order to arrest a fall.

An examination of belaying techniques indicates that it varies from country to country and with the type of mountaineering encountered. Basically the types of belay may be divided into DIRECT and INDIRECT and the method of belaying into STATIC and DYNAMIC. The direct belay is where the rope is used directly around a spike or tree the indirect belay is where the belayer is anchored and is holding the rope around his body to provide additional security and control of friction. The static belay is one which arrests a fall without allowing any rope movement and is only really applicable when a leader is belaying the second man from ABOVE. The dynamic belay requires the rope to slide under friction thereby absorbing some of the energy for the fall and reducing the force on the belayer and on the falling climber. A dynamic belay should always be used when the second man is belaying the leader. Gloves *must be worn* when using a dynamic belay to prevent friction burns.

DIRECT BELAYS
The direct static belay is a technique often used when climbers are roped up and moving together along a ridge where natural rock spikes provide a purchase for the rope. Moving together can be made more secure by flicking the rope in and out and over the spikes and pinnacles on ridges, by placing running belays and by the party members keeping as much as possible to different sides of the ridge. It is used on movement across snow and ice: in the snow the ice axe shaft is thrust into the snow surface and the rope paid out around the head; in ice the pick of the ice axe is driven into the ice surface and

the rope paid out over the top of the axe head. The great advantages of the direct static belay are the speed and relative simplicity with which it can be brought into operation. However, it is not efficient in holding leader falls and its use is best limited to safeguarding people climbing directly below the belayer.

The advent of mechanical belay devices and belay friction hitches which give a dynamic belay allow the direct belay to be used for belaying the leader. It is important to remember that with the direct belay the load comes *directly* onto the *anchor point* and it is consequently subjected to a greater loading than a properly executed indirect belay. When using the direct dynamic belay the belayer should be secured to a separate anchor point unless speed is important and the party is moving together (he may stop occasionally to give his partner a quick direct dynamic belay across a short difficult section). The hitch HMS Italian or belay plate used as a direct dynamic belay with the belayer anchored separately has the advantage of effectively separating the belayer from the belay system. In the event of a fall little strain comes onto the belayer and he is able to tie off and secure the second man and remove himself from the system. See diagram. In order to tie off the load rope a 5mm or 7mm sling can be attached to it using a prusik knot and the free end can be clipped into a separate anchor point. This can only be released by lifting the load to slacken the knot or by cutting the sling. A solution to this problem is to tie the end of the prusik sling onto the anchor karabiner with a mariner knot (diagram 3) which can be released under load. The direct dynamic belay can be used on snow using the ice axe foot brake and on ice using the ice piton foot brake. Both of these methods require considerable skill and practice to execute effectively and in both cases the belayer is in an unstable position in the event of anchor failure. A better belaying technique is to use a Saxon cross knot on the ice axe shaft or ice piton, as this eliminates the need of a boot for friction. The belayer faces into the snow slope with one hand braced on the head of the inserted ice axe and the other controlling the rope which normally has a minimum of 3 twists. This 'tripod position' has the advantage of being more stable than the boot axe position.

As a general rule on snow and ice the safest procedure would be to use indirect dynamic belays with mutiple anchor points whenever possible. It is important also to have a secure stance so that as much load as possible can be taken off the anchor points. Direct belays require *bomb proof* anchor points.

DIRECT SIMPLE TWIST AROUND A TREE
STATIC/DYNAMIC

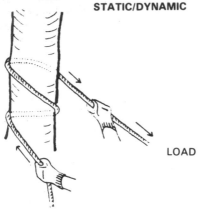

LOAD

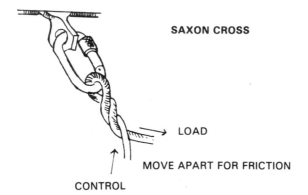

SAXON CROSS

LOAD

MOVE APART FOR FRICTION

CONTROL

This can be used on rock and ice pitons and around the shaft of an ice axe.

i.   Cannot be used on a flexible attachment point. i.e. sling or wire chock as the twists will transfer from the rope to the attachment point!

ii. Should only be used on anchor points which will withstand multi-directional forces.

DIRECT SPIKE BELAY - STATIC
N.B. will come off with upward pull

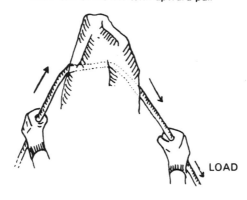

LOAD

ITALIAN OR MUNTER HITCH

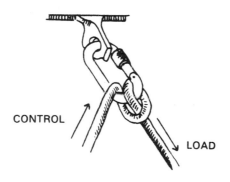

CONTROL

LOAD

i. Not suitable for use on Hawser laid rope.
ii. Should only be used on anchor points which will withstand multi-directional forces.

DIRECT BELAYS ON SNOW AND ICE

ICE AXE SHAFT BELAY (DIRECT)

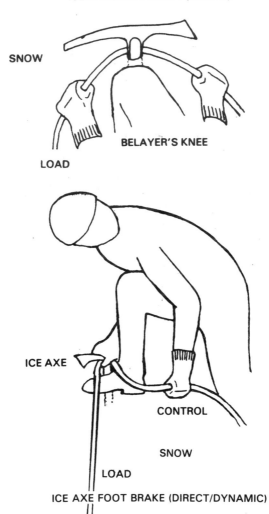

SNOW

BELAYER'S KNEE

LOAD

ICE AXE

CONTROL

SNOW

LOAD

ICE AXE FOOT BRAKE (DIRECT/DYNAMIC)

DIRECT BELAYS ON SNOW AND ICE

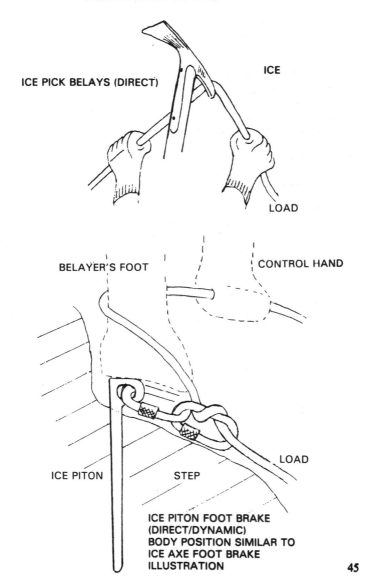

ICE PICK BELAYS (DIRECT)

ICE

LOAD

BELAYER'S FOOT

CONTROL HAND

ICE PITON

STEP

LOAD

ICE PITON FOOT BRAKE
(DIRECT/DYNAMIC)
BODY POSITION SIMILAR TO
ICE AXE FOOT BRAKE
ILLUSTRATION

INDIRECT BELAYS

The indirect belay involves the introduction of the climber into the belay chain between the anchor point and the moving climber. The indirect body belays can be divided into (i) The shoulder (ii) Waist/-Hip belay.

THE SHOULDER BELAY

The shoulder belay (page 48) is widely used by continental guides to safeguard their clients. These belays are static belays with the rope kept tight as the client climbs. The guide may or may not be anchored depending on the time factor and the situation. An experienced belayer can give considerable assistance to a struggling second: indeed I have seen a guide literally hoist a client up over a hard move. This method of belaying is easier to arrange than the waist belay if the belayer is wearing a rucksack. It is important not to lean forward when belaying, otherwise the rope will be pulled over the head and off the shoulder. This danger is decreased if the belayer is wearing a chest harness and is secured to a high anchor point. The directional loading of the belaying rope should be directly down not outwards as this is unstable. The body position should be:

1. Feet apart for stability.
2. Knee on load side locked and the foot firmly braced.
3. Shoulder braced against the rock face.
4. Both hands on the rope.

The shoulder belay is not suitable for a dynamic belay because:

i. There is not enough friction between the rope and the belayer's body.
ii. The point of loading is too high on the belayer.
iii. It is inefficient when subjected to an upward pull.

THE STOMPER BELAY

The stomper belay is useful on level glaciers or at the top of routes above the cornice. An ice screw or ice axe is placed vertically on the ice or snow and a karabiner attached through the eye hole. The live climbing rope is clipped up through the karabiner and the belayer stands on the anchor and adopts a shoulder belay. When the rope is loaded the full weight of the belayer is pulled down onto the anchors. It is important not to lean forward when using the belay otherwise the rope will be pulled off the shoulder.

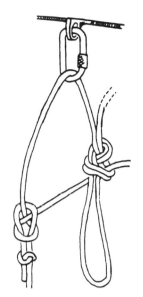

1. BELAY THROUGH THE WAIST LOOP TIED WITH FIGURE OF 8 ON BIGHT.

Pros: i) Belayer attached by doubled rope. ii) Belay easily adjustable.

CONS: i) Belayer tied into system—more difficult to escape. ii) Strain on waist tie bowline which must be locked off. iii) Strain on figure of 8 on bight by climbing rope if it is fully extended. iv) Nylon running on nylon during belaying.

2. BELAY FIGURE OF 8 BIGHT CLIPPED INTO ANCHOR KARABINER

Pros: i) Quick to tie. ii) Stronger than clove hitch. iii) Belayer not tied into system.

CONS: i) Not quick to adjust.
ii) Only one rope attaching belayer to anchor. iii) Strain on figure of 8 across the knot on full extension of climbing rope. iv) Nylon on nylon.

3. BELAY TIED WITH CLOVE HITCH ONTO ANCHOR KARABINER

PROS: i) Quick and simple to tie.
ii) Easily adjusted. iii) Belayer not tied into system.

CONS: i) Clove hitch weaker knot than figure of 8. ii) Only one rope attaching belayer to anchor. iii) Nylon on nylon. iv) Clove hitch can ride up onto gate -Screw sleeve desirable.

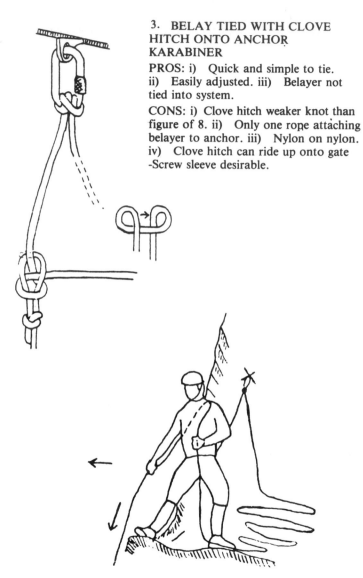

CLASSIC SHOULDER BELAY

THE WAIST/HIP BELAY

The waist/hip belay has been widely used as the standard indirect dynamic belay with minor technical differences in different places. The belaying rope may run over the top of the anchor rope in which case it is more difficult to arrest an upward pull arising from a leader fall with running belays. It is, however effective on downward pulls. An alternative is to run the belaying rope under the anchor rope so that an upward fall can more easily be arrested. In this case if no runners are in place or if runner failure occurs the rope is in an extremely difficult position to hold. A possible solution to this dilemma is to clip the belaying rope through a karabiner attached to the waist line thus securing it from a pull in either direction. This is awkward and time-consuming to arrange and may reduce the friction of the body belay. The position of the belaying hand on the rope may also vary according to the degree of friction required. In the U.K. it has been standard practice to have a twist of rope around the belay arm on the inactive side thus ensuring more body/rope contact and consequently more friction. It has a disadvantage, however, in that a full rope length fall may result in the belayer's arm being pulled around and trapped behind his back. This actually happened to a climber and he had to be rescued from his helpless position. The alternative method without a twist provides less friction but removes this danger. Gloves are essential for the safe operation of the waist/-hip belay.

The use of the waist/hip belay has important ramifications in the method of belaying attachment to the anchor and the following points should be noted. (Pages 50 and 51).

The introduction of a climbing belt or harness into the waist belay system solves some problems and creates others. The use of a canvas-sleeved climbing belt fastened by a safety buckle solves the problem of nylon running over nylon and the resulting danger of friction melting. The belayer can, in addition, remove himself from the system by undoing the belt as long as the tie back of the belay is to the karabiner and not directly into the belt. It is important when using the dynamic waist belay that the rope linking the anchor and the belayer be attached to the back or the side of the body. The normal tie in to the end of the rope or to the waist belt can easily be swivelled around to the back from the correct belay attachment position. When a harness with a fixed front attachment point is used a bight of the rope must be taken, tied off and clipped into a back waist loop. (See page 50). This modification is not necessary if belaying direct onto a separate anchor using an HMS Italian hitch. In this instance the climber can belay standing sideways tying into a separate anchor. Another solution is to belay with a HMS Italian hitch on a karabiner attached to the belayer's harness. This would be an indirect dynamic belay.

METHOD OF ANCHORING WHEN USING A HARNESS WITH A FRONT ATTACHMENT POINT

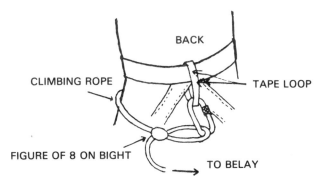

BACK

CLIMBING ROPE

TAPE LOOP

FIGURE OF 8 ON BIGHT

TO BELAY

PROS

1. Anchor attachment at rear.
2. Belayer can remove himself from the system by untying front attachment.

CONS

1. Awkward to arrange.
2. Slow.

ANCHORING USING A BIGHT OF ROPE TIED BACK TO THE WAISTLINE KRAB

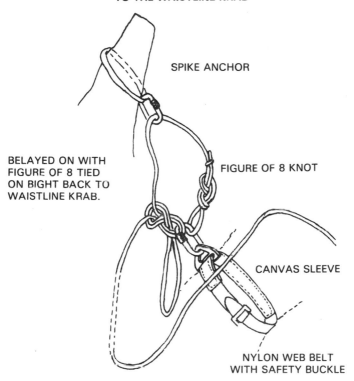

SPIKE ANCHOR

BELAYED ON WITH FIGURE OF 8 TIED ON BIGHT BACK TO WAISTLINE KRAB.

FIGURE OF 8 KNOT

CANVAS SLEEVE

NYLON WEB BELT WITH SAFETY BUCKLE

PROS
1. Belayer attached by double rope.
2. Easily adjustable when tied.
3. Rope runs over canvas sleeve not nylon on nylon.
4. Belayer can remove him/her self from the system by undoing belt whatever method of tying is used incorporating the waistline karabiner.

CONS
1. Strain on figure of 8 knot on bight by climbing rope if it is fully extended.

51

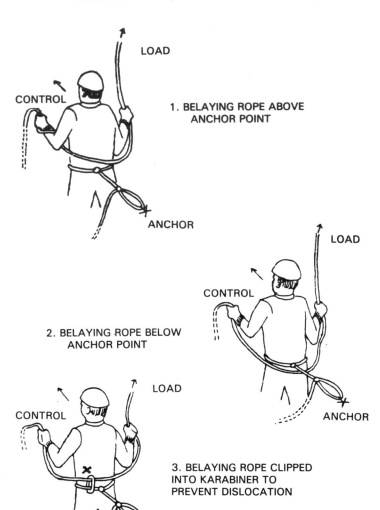

LOAD

CONTROL

1. BELAYING ROPE ABOVE ANCHOR POINT

ANCHOR

LOAD

CONTROL

2. BELAYING ROPE BELOW ANCHOR POINT

ANCHOR

LOAD

CONTROL

3. BELAYING ROPE CLIPPED INTO KARABINER TO PREVENT DISLOCATION

ANCHOR

CORRECT

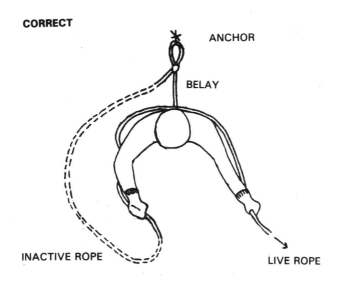

ANCHOR

BELAY

INACTIVE ROPE

LIVE ROPE

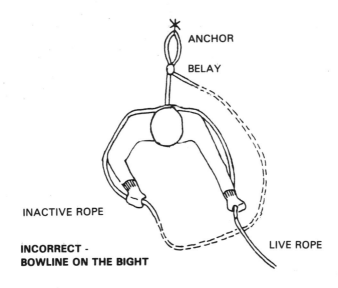

ANCHOR

BELAY

INACTIVE ROPE

LIVE ROPE

**INCORRECT -
BOWLINE ON THE BIGHT**

53

TAKING IN THE ROPE

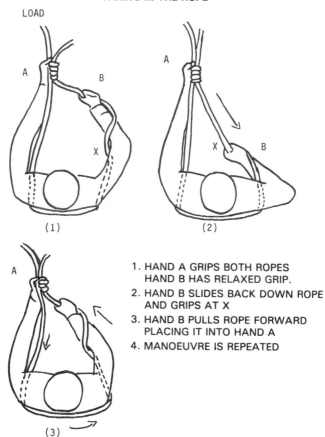

LOAD

(1)

(2)

(3)

1. HAND A GRIPS BOTH ROPES
   HAND B HAS RELAXED GRIP.
2. HAND B SLIDES BACK DOWN ROPE
   AND GRIPS AT X
3. HAND B PULLS ROPE FORWARD
   PLACING IT INTO HAND A
4. MANOEUVRE IS REPEATED

PAYING OUT — OPPOSITE HAND A PULLS ROPE THROUGH WHILE
HAND B ALLOWS ROPE TO RUN THROUGH
N.B. THE ROPE IS **ALWAYS** HELD IN BOTH HANDS

ITALIAN HITCH

METHOD I	METHOD II

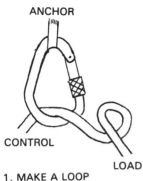

ANCHOR
CONTROL
LOAD

1. MAKE A LOOP

1. TWO LOOPS LIKE CLOVE HITCH

2. CLIP INTO KRAB

2. CLOSE LOOP X LIKE A BOOK ON LOOP Y

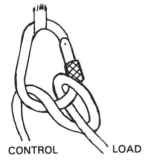

CONTROL   LOAD

3. CLOSE GATE AND SCREW SHUT

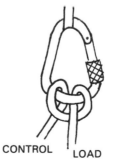

CONTROL   LOAD

3. CLIP KARABINER THROUGH TWO LOOPS

ITALIAN HITCH (Munter Hitch)

This simple friction hitch has become broadly accepted as a useful belaying method on kernmantel rope and may be used as a direct or indirect method of belaying. It has the great advantage of utilizing basic equipment, i.e. a karabiner and does not require the carrying of an extra gadget. There are two methods of tying the knot on a karabiner: (1) to assemble clip the rope through the karabiner, then take a loop on the load rope side, twist through ¼ turn and clip into the karabiner, (2) to assemble form two loops as in a clove hitch. The two loops are now bent forward like closing a book so they are touching side by side and the karabiner clipped through (see diagram). When using double rope, clip both ropes into the karabiner and into the runners unless you wish to keep them separate then you should use two separate karabiners.

It is important to realize that the mechanics of the friction hitch is such that the rope is only able to move in one direction. The hitch must invert when changing from paying out to taking in (or vice versa) and also when arresting a falling second. This rotation of the hitch is a limitation since it precludes karabiners with small openings and narrow sloping bases (D type) as the knot may jam on inversion. For the same reason it is also difficult to give a tight rope when using the knot. A large pear shaped screw gate karabiner is essential for the smooth operation of the hitch, e.g. the HMS twist lock karabiner. The braking action is different from the sticht plate (see chapter   ) which is a definite action of increasing friction by pulling the braking arm back and increasing the angle of the rope around the plate. The Italian hitch generates a large amount of friction by the rope passing over rope so is efficient with only a small amount of turn around the karabiner base. However, it should be noted that the braking effect is 30% less when the direction of pull is upwards - this will of course be compensated in part by the runner absorbing some of the fall energy. There was some concern over friction heating and possible damage to the rope but tests have shown this to be minimal and in any event a rope should be discarded after a severe fall. One problem which has arisen is that of rope twist resulting from falls stopped dynamically by the hitch and also from rappelling. This kinking may be due to the pulling of the rope over an edge in a slanting position to the rope axis. This kinking should be noted as a second possible limitation of the Italian hitch.

The braking force of the Italian hitch from the tests so far undertaken indicate that it gives a higher reading than the sticht plate

ITALIAN/MUNTER HITCH

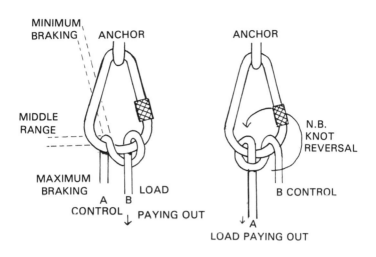

MINIMUM BRAKING

ANCHOR

MIDDLE RANGE

MAXIMUM BRAKING

A CONTROL

B LOAD

PAYING OUT

ANCHOR

N.B. KNOT REVERSAL

B CONTROL

A

LOAD PAYING OUT

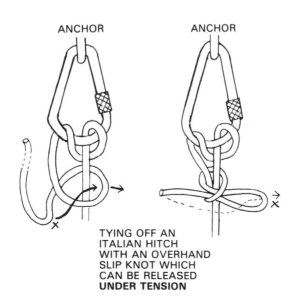

ANCHOR

ANCHOR

TYING OFF AN ITALIAN HITCH WITH AN OVERHAND SLIP KNOT WHICH CAN BE RELEASED **UNDER TENSION** especially on wet rope which appears to *increase* friction whereas on the sticht plate wet rope decreased friction. As with the sticht plate the hitch can be used on waist and chest as an indirect belay or as a direct belay on a multi directional anchor (bolt/piton). The knots can easily be locked off by tying an overhand slip knot which can be released under load.

THE FIGURE OF 8 BRAKE

The figure of 8 is one of the safest and foolproof of the descending devices and has increasingly been used as a belay device. In its normal mode of use with the rope threaded through in an S it gives a brake force of 110kg which is sufficient only for securing the second man on the rope with a top belay. Used with a cross over (see diagram 2) it gives a braking force of 215kg within the lower range of the HMS Italian Hitch and the Sticht Plate. (The Figure of 8 can also be utilized as an improvised sticht plate by using the small eye on the belay hole and tying the large eye back to the belay knot with a retaining cord). A limitation of the 8 in its normal use is that the bight of rope around the large eye can slip forward and cinch in a larks foot jamming the system.

The figure of 8 is best used for rappel situations where it can easily be tied off with an overhand slip knot or by jamming the control rope across and behind the loaded rope.

THE BANKL PLATE

The Bankl Plate is designed for use with two screw gate karabiners thus avoiding the problem of twisting. It has two modes of operation as shown in the diagrams as a rappel device and as a belay plate. As a belay plate its braking power is given as 190kg which is less than the HMS Italian hitch and the sticht plate and may be an advantage when belaying on snow and ice where more dynamic belays are required to reduce loading of anchors. Instructions for use are stamped on the plate. This device is not as wide as the sticht plate or HMS Italian hitch.

FIGURE OF 8 DESCENDER

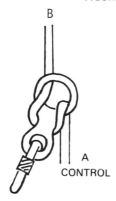

RAPPEL MODE
SINGLE ROPE
BRAKING FORCE 110Kg

LOCKED OFF
CONTROL ROPE CINCHED
ACROSS ROPE B

BELAY MODE
SONGLE ROPE
BRAKING FORCE 215Kg

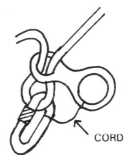

BELAY MODE
USED AS A STICHT PLATE
BRAKING FORCE 215Kg

BANKL PLATE

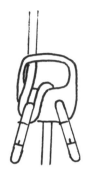

RAPPEL SINGLE ROPE

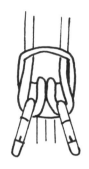

RAPPEL DOUBLE ROPE

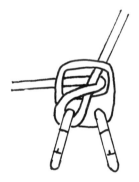

BELAY MODE
190Kg BRAKING FORCE

KARABINER
EYEHOLES

BANKL PLATE

CHAPTER III
BELAYING 2
THE STICHT BELAY PLATE*
GENERAL POINTS ON BELAYING

It was inevitable with the increasing technological innovations which are at present affecting climbing that eventually an effective dynamic belay device would be developed. At the present time the energy absorption capacity of modern climbing ropes is measured by the impact force, i.e. the maximum force to which a climber is exposed when falling onto the rope. The Union Internationale des Association d'Alpinisme, an international body which sets standards for climbing equipment, requires an impact force of 1200Kg (approx. 2640lbs.) for 11mm ropes and 600Kg (approx. 1320lbs.) for 9mm ropes. What this means is that if a static belay is used, i.e. no rope movement allowed during a fall, this is the maximum force which will be exerted by the belay chain. Dynamic belaying absorbs part of the fall energy by gradually arresting the fall, i.e. by permitting a length of reserve rope to slide past the belay point. It is, of course, essential to have an adequate reserve of rope to ensure effective dynamic belaying. When one is climbing 150' pitches the 165' rope allows for a dynamic belay.

The traditional method of belaying is the dynamic hip or waist belay which requires considerable practice to execute properly. In addition, it suffers from the following drawbacks:

i.   It is often difficult to arrange using a climbing harness which has a fixed attachment point at the front. The belayer needs to be anchored from the rear in order to properly execute the waist belay. This problem did not arise when climbers tied onto the end of the rope directly or used a swami belt both of which allow the attachment point (of the climbing rope) to be swivelled to the back of the belayer.

ii.   It is extremely difficult to hold a long fall when no running belays have been placed.

iii. In hot weather the absence of clothing greatly increases the possibility of rope burns to the belayer.

iv.   Light climbers, i.e. small men and women, experience greater difficulty in belaying heavy climbers.

v.   There is a danger that the rope can be yanked completely away from the belayer.

61

---

* The Sticht Belay Plate was the first of many belay devices which conform to the same basic principles. The information in this chapter could apply to most of the current popular belay devices.

vi.   The possibility exists of the nylon climbing rope running across the belay attachment which is nylon and causing friction melting. To a certain extent this can be avoided by padding the back of the belay with clothing to avoid nylon running on nylon.

The Sticht plate is a simple lightweight device designed to give effective and controlled dynamic belaying and at the same time removing many of the above disadvantages of the conventional waist/hip dynamic belay. It consists of an aluminium plate ⅜ins. thick and 2⅜ins. in diameter with two slots, one for 9mm rope and one for 11mm rope (models with one slot for single 11mm and two slots for double 9mm are also available - probably the most versatile in use is the 9mm/11mm plate). When using the brake plate in conjunction with a harness with a front attachment point the belayer stands 45° to the rock facing out and towards the direction of the lead climber. He is anchored directly from his front attachment point to the rock face. The sticht plate is attached to the belayer's harness by a short piece of nylon cord not less than 6-8ins. long. A loop of rope is then passed through the slot and into a locking screw karabiner which is clipped into the rope loop formed by tying into the harness. The rope is paid out and taken in with one hand holding the active rope leading to the climber and the other hand holding the inactive rope which leads back eventually to the belayer. A fall is held by drawing back the inactive rope opposite to the possible direction of the fall forcing the plate back against the locking screw karabiner. The hand behind the plate has a braking and holding function and should be protected by a leather palmed glove, the braking should be instinctive. i.e. as firmly as possible and not with a gradual increase in pressure since the plate itself automatically applies the dynamic element when loaded.

It is important to maintain the distance of 3 to 6ins. between the plate and the locking screw karabiner when paying out and taking in the rope. If the plate is drawn up hard against the karabiner the rope may become blocked and the position of the plate has to be corrected by the free hand. This problem is solved by using a plate with a strong steel spring which holds the brake plate away from the karabiner except when a strong force is applied. It is desirable to use an oval rather than a D-shaped karabiner to provide an even surface for the spring to ride against. The spring does reduce the likelihood of unwanted blocking of the rope but also has a tendency to tangle into other pieces of climbing gear, i.e. slings. In order to reduce this occurence a clip is fitted on the plate to retain the spring when not in use. In order to facilitate quick removal of the plate to use on a direct belay the nylon retaining cord is often clipped into a second karabiner on the belayer's harness. I have replaced this cord with a swaged loop of stainless steel wire which can be clipped directly into the belaying karabiner with no danger of friction melting from the moving rope. This removes the necessity of a second karabiner, is quick and easy to use and so far has proved to be very effective.

The braking force of the Sticht plate can be varied between 460lbs. to 1000lbs. by using it in conjunction with a waist belay and/or with two belay karabiners rather than one. The braking stages are as follows:-

STAGE I	Sticht Plate and one karabiner	WET ROPE	No figure available	290lbs.
		DRY ROPE	Approximately	490lbs.
STAGE II	Sticht Plate and one karabiner with body belay	WET ROPE	"	510lbs.
		DRY ROPE	"	730lbs.
STAGE III	Sticht Plate and two karabiners	WET ROPE	"	660lbs.
		DRY ROPE	"	880lbs.
STAGE IV	Sticht Plate and two karabiners with body belay	WET ROPE	"	880lbs.
		DRY ROPE	"	1100lbs.

The figures given are from the Salewa information brochure on the Sticht plate. No figure was given on the brake's performance with a wet rope in STAGE I. This figure is interpolated with the 200lbs. difference between wet and dry ropes in other stages.

As a general rule the higher the figure the greater the force exerted on the belay chain. Therefore, when belaying on snow and ice, i.e. where anchors offer less holding power, the methods giving the lower figures should be used. Where a long fall with no runners is anticipated and there is little reserve inactive rope then methods giving the higher figures can be used as there will be minimal rope passing through the plate. Stage IV functions almost as a static belay if it is used with a low fall factor* hence the impact force on the belay chain will be high. In modern climbing with frequent running belays, stage I is adequate with stage II and III applicable when the rope is wet. Stage IV has justification if the belayer prepares to hold a hard fall on the wet rope without running belay above the belay position. It is obvious that even with a Sticht plate the running belays are an essential part of the belay chain and it should be standard procedure to place a running belay as soon as possible after leaving the belay stance.

If the leader uses more running belays to reduce the length of fall, the fall factor will continue to be reduced and the fall will be softened.

* Definition of Fall Factor: This describes the severity of the fall.

$$\text{Fall Factor} = \frac{\text{Length of Fall}}{\text{Rope run out}}$$

Example   10 metres lead out above belay results in a 20 metre fall. $^{20}/_{10} = 2$ Fall Factors. This is the highest fall factor possible.

Example   10 metres lead out above belay; runner placed at 5 metres results in a 10 metre fall (5 x 2) $^{10}/_{10} = 1$ Fall Factor.

The procedure for double rope technique using the Sticht Plate is the same as for the single rope. The two ropes are passed through the Sticht plate, one rope through each slot and both are clipped into a single oval locking scew karabiner which is fastened to the rope attachment loop. The hands and fingers hold the ropes in such a way that either one of the ropes can be paid out or taken in separately or together as required. When using two ropes in lead climbing they should be clipped singly and alternately into the running belay points so that only one rope is loaded in the event of a fall. If no running belays are used or if both ropes are clipped into a single running belay the braking effect will be Stage I - 490 x two = 980lbs. When using double rope with no running belays and a low braking effect is required, this may be attained by:

i.   Clipping the second rope out of the belay plate (only if the first rope is 11mm).

ii.   Unevenly feeding out the ropes so that both ropes would not be simultaneously stressed by a fall. The Sticht plate automatically separates the double ropes facilitating rope management in double rope technique.

The Sticht plate can also be used as a direct belay, i.e. it can be operated, attached to an independent anchor point. This anchor point should be capable of withstanding multi-directional forces, i.e. it should be a piton, expansion bolt or secure thread belay. There

THE STICHT BELAY PLATE

STAGE 1. 1 KRAB

STAGE 2. 1 KRAB & BODY BELAY

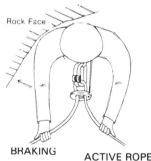

Rock Face

BRAKING

ACTIVE ROPE

BRAKING   ACTIVE ROPE

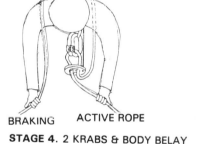

Rock Face

BRAKING   ACTIVE ROPE

STAGE 3. 2 KRABS

BRAKING   ACTIVE ROPE

STAGE 4. 2 KRABS & BODY BELAY

STAGE 1. FREE MOVEMENT FOR BRAKING ARM — CORRECT
STAGE 3. FREE MOVEMENT FOR BRAKING ARM — INCORRECT
ROPE SHOULD BE REVERSED AND BELAYED AS IN 1

should be a second anchor point for the belayer. When using the plate as a direct belay on a separate anchor point it is important to be close enough to pull the inactive rope into the full braking position whatever the direction of loading. The advantage of the direct belay is that a fallen climber can be tied off to the belay point and the belayer remains free to undertake further action. There are various ways of tying off a fallen climber to the sticht plate by:

i.   Tying an overhand slip knot of the inactive rope around the active rope: this can easily be released even when loaded.

ii.   Tying a clove hitch behind the loaded Sticht plate which can also be released under load.

iii. Fastening a prusik knot on a sling in front of the plate on the load rope and tying it off to an anchor.

Further considerations when using the Sticht plate:

1.   The positioning of oneself in relation to the cliff is important to ensure there is freedom of the braking arm to move back and apply friction on the brake plate. When a climbing partner leads through and crosses over in front of the belayer the alignment of the rope in the brake may require changing to avoid the possibility of the braking arm being jammed against the rock face. See Stage I and Stage III.

2.   Care must also be taken when fingers are near an active Sticht plate otherwise injury could occur if one is caught in the brake.

3.   Do not permit loose clothing or the retaining cord to be near the brake whilst belaying as they may be dragged into the brake and block it reducing its dynamic effect.

4.   It is important to avoid tangling or kinking of the rope as these may jam the Sticht plate and prevent its smooth operation.

Apart from its use as a belay device the Sticht plate can also be used for lowering and rappeling with the suggested modification of inserting the back of a second knob between the brake knob and the belay plate (Steve Reid). This provides more metal to dissipate friction heat and also gives a smooth run through of the rope reducing the jerkiness which may strain the anchors. The Sticht plate can also be used for ascending the rope - first attach a prusik sling to the rope above the Sticht plate and transfer your body weight to the foot loop provided. When the climber is standing in the prusik sling he is able to take up the slack through the Sticht plate (removing additional rappel karabiner) and move it up the rope. He then holds his body weight on the plate with one hand and moves the prusik sling up the rope.

LOCKING OFF A STICHT PLATE — WITH PRUSIK AND MARINER

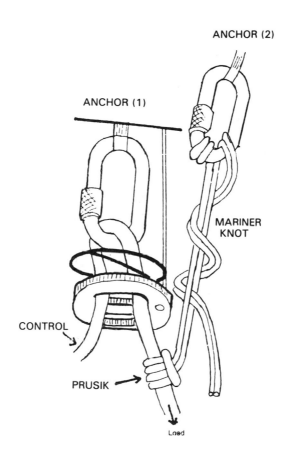

ANCHOR (2)

ANCHOR (1)

MARINER KNOT

CONTROL

PRUSIK

Load

LOCKING OFF A STICHT PLATE - WITH HALF HITCH ON THE BIGHT

ANCHOR (1)

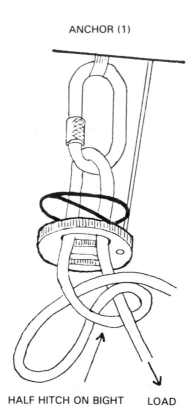

HALF HITCH ON BIGHT   LOAD

There is little doubt that the Sticht plate is an efficient dynamic belay device which when used properly will give good service to rock climbers and mountaineers. It has been adopted by Glenmore Lodge and Plas-y-Brenin in the U.K. and is used in Europe. There are other belay plates working on a similar principle: the Clog Cosmic Arrester and the DMM Bettabrake which indicates to me the effectiveness of the technique. However, the basic skill of the waist belay should not be forgotten as it is useful where the Sticht plate is not applicable - in hawser laid ropes or on frozen sheath rope.

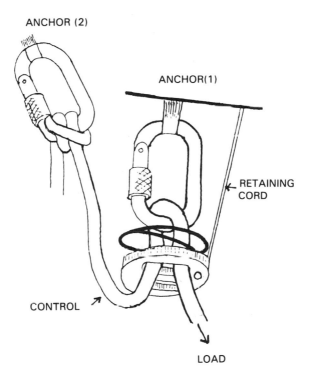

**LOCKING OFF A STICHT PLATE —
WITH A CLOVE HITCH**

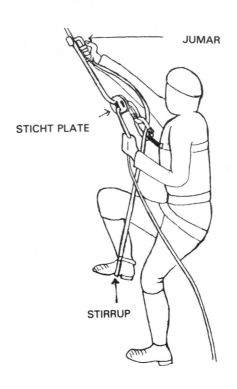

JUMAR

STICHT PLATE

STIRRUP

ASCENDING USING A STICHT PLATE

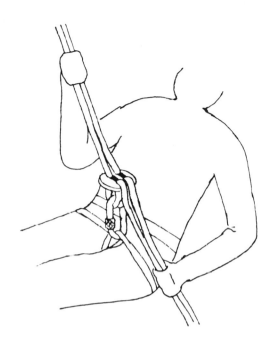

RAPPELLING USING A STICHT PLATE
Note the ropes are automatically separated.

FURTHER POINTS ON BELAYING

The U.I.A.A. list the following essential requirements for belaying:

1. It should be safe to the belayer and the falling climber.
2. Simple and quick to apply on wet, dry and icy rock.
3. Suitable for single or double ropes, paying out and taking in.
4. A controllable braking force on all falls in all directions.
5. Possible to lock off the rope after holding a fall and the belayer detach himself from the belay chain.

Three desirable requirements were that gloves were unnecessary, standard equipment should be used and that they were adaptable for lowering and rappeling. Practice of basic belaying skills under simulated fall conditions is essential to develop belaying competency. There is NO SUBSTITUTE for this practice.

THE BELAY STANCE

Each stance and belay is a unique situation which the climber must examine to the best mechanical advantage. Few are perfect but with the application of a few basic rules, they can be made more secure.

i. Use two anchors wherever possible - when you arrive at a stance select your anchors - two about 3 feet apart for stability. Tie on to one and adjust the bight of tied off rope so it clips into the second anchor point. Take up a stance in such a position that the tension is equally divided between the anchor points and both tie ins are tight.

ii. ABC - Anchor, Belayer, Climber are in a straight line in the direction of anticipated force - remember runner placements result in an upward pull and a downward counteracting belay may be necessary to arrange especially if the anchors are not multi directional.

iii. Length - Tie in to belay anchor: long belay tie in should be used with care as they are liable to sideways instability and to stretching. Always keep back from the edge of the stance and make a generous allowance for belay stretch.

iv. Stability, - a sitting belay offers more stability than a standing belay stance.

v. Tight on belay. Always ensure there is no slack in the belay tie in to prevent yourself being pulled off balance.

CHAPTER IV

THE RUNNING BELAY
ANCHORS: ROCK/SNOW/ICE

THE RUNNING BELAY

No single factor has played a more important part in the development of really high standard free climbing than the technical development of the running belay. In the early days of mountaineering, climbers often untied the rope and threaded it behind chockstones to give themselves protection. Nowadays, the modern climber has a vast and often confusing array of weaponry to choose from when he requires protection. The purpose of this chapter is to examine the different types of protection available and to look at placement techniques and other factors which control the usage of running belays.

The primary function of the running belay is to protect the leader in the event of a fall by reducing the distance he descends. The severity of a fall is measured by the FALL FACTOR: this is obtained by dividing the length of the fall by the length of rope run out. e.g. A climber leading out 20 feet of rope placing no running belays falls 40 feet giving a fall factor of 2 (40/20). This is the maximum fall factor and is reached every time whatever distance the climber falls up to the full length of the rope if he does not place any running belays. Although the severity of a fall is constant the longer the fall the longer the impact time e.g. the longer the force acts on the belay chain. Therefore, falls should be kept as short as possible. The introduction of the running belay into the climbing chain has dramatic effects on the fall factor and the impact time. Both are reduced. A climber leading out 20 feet and falls off having placed a runner at 10 feet, experiences a fall of 20 feet and a fall factor of 1 (20/20). He falls only 20 feet rather than 40 feet and the impact time is correspondingly reduced.

1). The First Runner Rule is to place a runner as soon as it is feasible after setting out from the stance and belay. As a general rule the harder and steeper the climb the greater the propensity to use runners. In practise it is advisable to runner up the easier climbs as well as there is more likelihood of injury during a fall in the more broken easy climb than a vertical wall.

A modern (11mm) climbing rope is designed to absorb the energy generated by the fall and to have an impact force of 1200kg. This is the maximum impact force the belayer will be subjected to. However, when a runner is introduced into the system it is subjected to double the impact force 2 x 1200kg = (5280lbs). The heaviest load through the system is therefore placed on the running belay and consequently, the Second Runner Rule is (2) The runners should be capable of withstanding twice the maximum impact force 2 x 2400kg whenever possible. In practise, dynamic belaying, rope friction, and knot slippage absorb some of the energy and this force is rarely fully

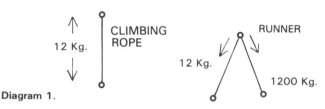

Diagram 1.

exerted on the running belay. However, in the runner chain there should always be some *full strength runners. (3) The Third Basic Runner Rule is that the components of the runner chain - the sling or rope, the knot and the karabiner should be of uniform strength as the strength of the runner is the strength of its weakest link.

* This term applies to the impact force x 2 as an index of full strength.

Ethical Considerations of Runner Placement
Having established the basic rules governing runners the question arises, how many should you use and when should you place them? The number of runners carried and used on a pitch depends on personal preference and availability of placement on the climb. In the modern era of free climbing most people carry a wide selection of running belays and use them frequently, 10-15 feet being an average distance. It is possible to overprotect a pitch by placing too many runners so they get in the way of holds and the climber is tempted to use them as aid. In the current ethics a running belay is for protection only although five stages of usage can be distinguished, each one progressively less ethical and less desirable.

1. Protection - conventional use
2. Resting - clipping in and resting on a tight rope
3. Tension - used as partial aid to complete a move
4. Direct Aid - used directly to assist upward progress
5. Point of Retreat - when unable to complete the pitch

May also be used in conjunction with the Yoyo technique -alternate leads of same pitch placing progressively higher runners until pitch is overwhelmed by this joint effort. Mention should also be made here of the preplaced runner placed on a top rope or from a rappel, an increasingly common practice on high standard first ascents. This 'technique?' allows the aspiring first ascensionist (1) to conserve energy in placing the runner, (2) have a sneak reconnaissance of the line, and (3) terrifies the poor guy who does the on-sight second ascent.

Dynamic Considerations of Runner Placement

A good climber is one who anticipates possibilities and evaluates the likelihood of their occurrence. He is constantly monitoring his actions and results, maintaining at the same time, a high state of awareness. This to me, is one of the exacting and exciting aspects of the sport. Such an approach is of great importance when using running belays. The climber must give consideration to his direction of fall when he places a runner and also the resulting direction of pull on the second. If the lead climber has climbed up and traversed to the side and then placed a runner then the direction of pull will be diagonally up and the belayer should change his position accordingly. If this is not done there is a danger of the belayer being

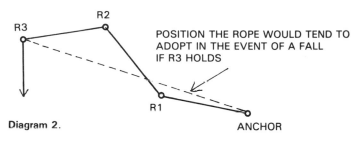

Diagram 2.

pulled off his stance if it is a small one and even being injured by being pulled against projecting rock. Care should be exercised when belaying in natural sentry boxes and alcoves. It is essential that the belay anchors be multi-directional. I remember an incident when early in my climbing career I fell, was held by a runner, and pulled my second off his spike belay and up into the air. We were both hanging from a 5mm line runner! The placement of each runner will have an effect on the previous placement and in the event of a fall the climbing rope will straighten under load tending to dislodge runners. See diagram 2. It is possible to minimize this danger by placing runners in as straight a line as possible and by lengthening each runner with a tape or rope sling if it is a wire. This will also help reduce rope drag which can be a problem on long pitches. The use of double rope technique will also help minimize rope drag. The same technique is also used when climbing over overlaps and overhangs which have protection points below them - attach a long sling so the climbing rope runs clear of the rock.

Rope Position and Runner Placement

This is really using runners to control the position and the direction of the rope and can be very useful in the following situations.

i.   Placing a runner to move the rope away from a sharp edge which could abrade or cut it.

ii. Placing a runner in order to prevent the rope jamming in a deep crack.

Further Considerations of Runner Placement

When teaching a friend or instructing, the running belay can often be used to indicate the line of the route especially if route finding is difficult. It is also inadvisable to place runners which are awkward and difficult to remove in strenuous places as consideration should be given to the second. A good practice to follow is to place runners before and after difficult moves. One must also consider the protection of the second man especially on traverses as the runners may offer poor protection for the second.

The safest solution would be to utilize two ropes clipping one in across the traverse and leaving one free to protect the second.

There is little doubt that the development of improved belaying techniques in conjunction with improved methods of protection, has greatly increased the standard of free climbing. Attitudes also appear to have changed - taking a fall is no longer regarded as such a serious event because of the high safety factor which has been built into the modern rock climbing system. In the early days of rock climbing with direct belays and hemp ropes a fall often involved serious consequences. It may be that the fundamental nature of the sport is changing and the degree of risk decreasing, as no attempt to push technical standards higher in comparative safety, will equal the degree of commitment accepted and practiced by the pioneers.

PROTECTING A TRAVERSE

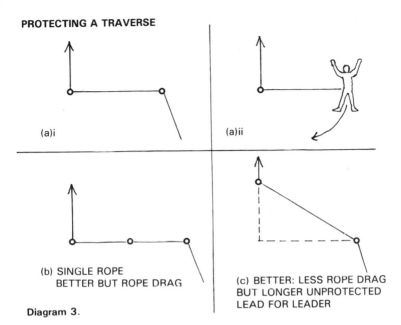

(a)i

(a)ii

(b) SINGLE ROPE
    BETTER BUT ROPE DRAG

(c) BETTER: LESS ROPE DRAG
    BUT LONGER UNPROTECTED
    LEAD FOR LEADER

Diagram 3.

ANCHORS - ROCK, SNOW & ICE

The most important single factor in any rescue situation is the provision of sound anchor points. In the current trends of clean climbing the less the environmental impact the greater the acceptability of the anchor points. Applying this criteria it is possible to come up with the following acceptable anchors on rock.

1. Natural Anchors - thread, natural chockstones, spikes
2. Chocks -
3. Pitons -
4. Bolts -

It is interesting to note that the ethic of clean climbing excludes pitons and bolts which are technically strong anchors capable of withstanding multi-directional forces. It is highly desirable in the modern system of belaying to have multi-directional main anchors.

Natural Anchors

Natural anchors are rock spikes, natural chockstones jammed into cracks, natural threads and trees. All natural anchors should be examined, tested physically and audibly, hitting or tapping to ascertain that they are solid. Loose anchors and hollow sounding anchors should be avoided. Large detached boulders and small trees should be treated with caution as should trees that show signs of decay. When necessary always use back up anchors and never hesitate to use artificial anchors if the need arises - remember it is your life. Thread and good chockstone anchors are multi-directional, i.e. can withstand a pull in any direction and are consequently safer anchor points.

Chocks

In the current trend of clean climbing the less the environmental impact the greater the acceptability of the anchor points. Applying this criteria it is possible to compile the following list. An often forgotten consequence of the 'clean climbing fashion' is that it excludes anchors, pitons and bolts which are capable of withstanding multi-directional forces. The use of all chock protection requires careful placement if one is to avoid unzipping pitches. It is interesting to see the technological development of chocks which have taken place within the current ethical constraints. For the purpose of this chapter I shall only deal with artificial chocks as running belays.

CHOCKS

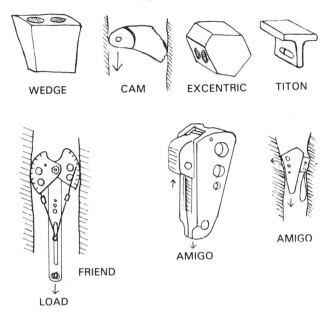

WEDGE   CAM   EXCENTRIC   TITON

FRIEND

LOAD

AMIGO

AMIGO

i.   Natural anchors - thread-multi directional, spikes - uni-directional, and natural chockstones - could be either
ii.   Chocks - uni-directional
iii.   Pitons - multi-directional
iv.   Bolts - multi-directional

The first chocks were pebbles of natural stone which were carried by climbers and inserted into cracks. These were augmented by jammed knots where the knot tying the sling was used as a chock. Then brass and steel nuts were drilled out to remove the thread and placed on rope slings to replace the inserted pebbles. Finally came the light alloy chock which was specifically manufactured for climbing protection. The initial form was the wedge which was used in much the same way as the inserted chockstone. With the development of this aluminium chock the climbers 'rack' of hardwear expanded as the drilled out nuts and sundry plumber's joints were replaced by sets of machined aluminium.

The next step forward was the development of the excentric by Chouinard which was capable of being used for 3 width placements and also had a camming action in parallel sided cracks. These versatile chocks have dominated the climbing scene until quite recently. The introduction of the single cam nut, some of which are spring loaded, did not have a great impact on anchor placements. The single cam is versatile in that it can be used for variable width placements and theoretically should be easier to remove than wedges.

The development of Titon by Bill Forrest was a radical change in design from the conventional solid or compact nut. The revolutionary T shape had wedging and camming capabilities as well as the possibility of using the flanges for placements in natural slots where conventional placements are not always possible. Titons are made in a full range of sizes from one to seventeen covering a range of cracks from $7/16''$ to $7''$ wide. It is in the upper sizes that the Titon is really useful since it is easier to carry and rack and does not take up a lot of space since it is long and narrow. Weight for weight the Titon slung with tape is lighter than hexes slung with cordage. The interesting fact concerning the Titons is that they require a change in attitude of thinking of the climber. It is not just a matter of looking, electing and slotting; a little more skill is required in the placement and it was a little time before I was placing Titons as quickly as I placed conventional nuts. The increased versatility is well worth the extra time and effort required for complete mastery of usage. Whatever type of chock is used it is interesting to note that in the very small sizes manufacturers revert to the wedge design, probably because the small chock size and the necessity for wire threads preclude the use of camming designs.

The techniques of stacking chocks to fit on extra large cracks is sometimes used when arranging runner protection. Properly executed this is a useful technique but it does require skill and practice. It is important to remember to always load the upper camming chock as this keeps the 'stacked chocks' together. Simond have actually designed their chocks to slot into each other to facilitate stacking giving a superior arrangement to improvised stacking. One of the most effective stacking techniques is to use an inverted wedge against an upright wedge giving a very secure stacking arrangement. Stacking is probably used more in aid climbing than in providing conventional runner placements. In free climbing it is always desirable to carry what you need for adequate protection. Tube chocks or Bongs used as chocks can also provide protection in extra large cracks and the latter can be also stacked to give a greater range of placements. However, both are rather bulky to carry and take up a great deal of space on a climbers rack. Probably the best chock for outsize cracks are the larger size Titons.

The most radical technological advance in chocks has been the development of the double spring loaded cam nuts known as Friends. This nut is capable of instant placement in parallel sided cracks. The cams are retracted by using your index finger and second finger on the trigger bar whilst supporting the stem with your thumb like using a syringe. As with all equipment, care must be taken in placement to ensure the stem is aimed in the direction of loading and the crack is not too wide or too flared for secure placement.

However much technology develops to facilitate the climbing process it will fortunately never completely supplant the skill and judgement of the individual. Tests as to the efficacy of different types of chocks are meaningless as the act of placement is the most important factor. It is the responsibility of the individual climber to develop his skill with his own equipment so he is using it to its optimum advantage. This is done by practice and experience, over a long period of time.

Factors to Consider in Chock Placement
1. Configuration of the crack
2. Soundness of the walls of the crack
3. Correct size of chock for the crack
4. Placement - seating of the chock - well seated/secure
5. Direction of loading

CHOCK A BLOCK CHOCKS

TYPE	ACTION	PLACE-MENTS	STACKING	COMMENTS
Wedge	Wedge	2 Width	Yes	Essential in very small cracks. Widely used.
Excentric	Wedge Cam	3 Width	Yes	Unwieldy in large sizes.
Titon	Wedge Cam	Variable Range	Yes	Versatile. Excellent in very large sizes. Requires placement practice.
Single Cam Nut	Cam	Variable Range	No	Some types spring loaded.
Friends	Spring Loaded Cam	Variable Range	No	Quick to place, and may become essential part of extremely high standard face climbing.
Tube Chocks	Wedge (Cam?)	3 Width	?	Tendency to rotate unless notched. Bulky to carry on rack.
Bongs	Wedge (Cam?)	3 Width	Yes	Bulky to carry.
Amigo	Wedge Spring Loaded	Variable Range	Possibly	Very recent development.

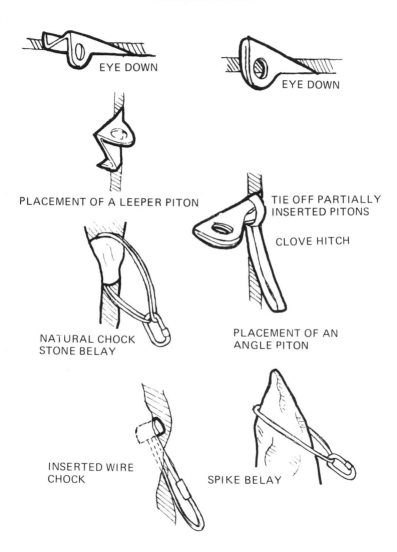

EYE DOWN

EYE DOWN

PLACEMENT OF A LEEPER PITON

TIE OFF PARTIALLY
INSERTED PITONS

CLOVE HITCH

NATURAL CHOCK
STONE BELAY

PLACEMENT OF AN
ANGLE PITON

INSERTED WIRE
CHOCK

SPIKE BELAY

Pitons

There are two types of pitons; hard steel or chrome molybdenum pitons, which do not bend and hold by wedging in the placement cracks, and soft steel, which follow the line of the crack. Soft steel pitons are often found as 'fixed pitons' and some authorities recommend them for use in limestone rock which is rather soft for hard steel pegs. The hard steel pitons on the market are generally well designed, with heads which lie flush to the rock when hammered home and with gradual, rather than sharp tapers. There are various designs to cover a wide range of cracks, from very thin and hairline cracks, to cracks over 6 inches in width. The thinner pitons are designed for aid climbing only. The basic designs for the wider cracks are:-

i. Leepers, which have a 'Z' shaped profile and are placed in vertical cracks with the eye uppermost and in horizontal cracks with the eye down.

ii. Angles, which have 'V' shaped profiles and are placed with the eye down in horizontal cracks. Both types of pitons are placed so the edges bite into the side of the crack. The angles grade into bongs as they increase in size.

Placement of Pitons

When placing pitons always choose the crack which gives the best mechanical advantage, e.g. horizontal cracks sloping slightly downwards into the rock. Avoid blind cracks, shattered areas, downward sloping cracks in roofs and overhangs, cracks which open out above and below the piton position. The correct piton to use is one which will enter two thirds of the way in without hammering. If it is too big, do not overdrive, but tie off with a sling in a clove hitch. Always sling the piton if there is any danger of the karabiner acting as a lever and make sure the gate of the karabiner is pointing down. If the pitons you have are too small for the cracks available you may be able to stack them. Leepers are the best pegs to insert together and stack. Stacking is used mainly in aid climbing and should only be used in main belays when there is no alternative. In winter cracks are often choked with ice and pitons with channels, e.g. Leepers and angles are the most effective as the ice can be extruded via the channels as the piton is inserted.

At the present time, there is growing opposition to the use of hard steel pitons as their repeated use scars the rock. Whenever possible chocks or fixed pitons should be used to minimize damage to the rock.

BOLT ANCHORS

COMPRESSION BOLT
GRANITE RAWL DRILL

HANGER

BOLT   SELF DRIVE SLEEVE   WEDGE

SELF DRIVE
EXPANSION BOLT.
LIMESTONE

½" ANGLE IN ⅜" DRILL HOLE
SANDSTONE

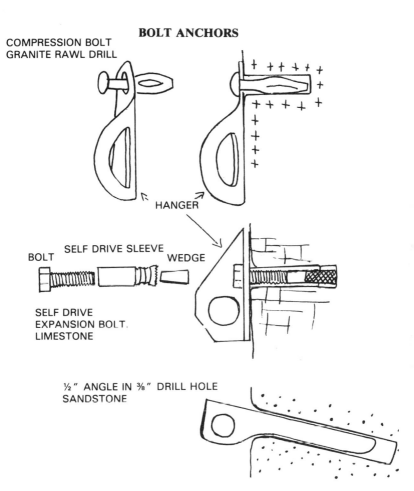

Bolts

Bolts are permanent anchors which are normally placed by drilling holes with a percussion tool. There are many different types on the market, however, there are two basic designs. Hangers are attached to the bolts to provide karabiner attachment points.

i. The self driving expansion bolt usually used in limestone and requiring a special placement tool.

ii. The compression bolt which is placed in a hole made by a rawl drill. This type of bolt is squeezed or compressed into the drill hole by hammering and is normally used on limestone.

A third bolt or piton bolt is used on soft sandstone where ½" angle pitons are hammered into ⅜" drill holes. The hard steel bites into the soft rock to give a reasonable anchor.

The use of bolts is restricted to places where there is a complete absence of any possible alternative anchor.

Functions to consider in bolt placement:

1. Only in solid continuous rock not detached blocks.
2. Drill vertically and square to the rock surface.
3. Clean/blow out drill hole to remove dust.
4. Always drill an adequate depth.
5. Do not overdrive.

Testing Insitu Anchors: Never assume an insitu anchor is secure.

1. Chocks - visually and physically by wiggling and tugging.
2. Pitons - tap with hammer - rising ring indicates sound placement, dull sound indicates poor placement. Check if any movement to and fro along crack line.
3. Bolts. Do not tap bolts. Inspect visually and clip in sling and test by pulling.

ANCHORS ON SNOW AND ICE

Whenever possible rock anchors should be sought for as they are far superior to any snow or ice belay. However, this is not always possible and other methods have to be employed.

Snow Anchors

1. **Deadman** (Fig.1. page 88)

    The most effective anchor on snow is the deadman. This consists of a flat alloy plate about one foot square with a four foot wire sling attached to its centre. A 'T' shaped slot is cut in the snow slope with care being taken not to disturb the snow on the down slope side. The plate is then inserted at an angle of about 40 degrees to the snow slope. This angle is obtained by placing an ice axe perpendicular to the slope and bisecting the angle between the shaft and the slope with the deadman; cast the deadman plate back a few degrees from this. Attach another sling to the wire sling to give a length of at least 6 feet and pull it tight in the centre slot. The sling should exit at the end of the slot. Check the depth of the deadman, using the ice axe to measure the distance from the wire attachment point to the surface of the snow. Cut a stance below the sling and belay in the normal way. Check that the deadman is 'seated' by pulling tight on the belay. Avoid placing the deadman between two snow layers of different hardness.

In the absence of a deadman a sling may be clove hitched around the shaft of a strong ice axe shaft and the axe buried in the horizontal position in a 'T' shaped slot. A shovel, ski, or piece of board may also be used. (Fig.4. page 88).

2. **Snow Mushroom** (Fig.2. page 88).
   Another quite effective anchor in hard snow is a snow mushroom. This is a bollard cut out of snow with the size depending on the hardness of the snow - 3 or 4 feet across is usually sufficient. The climbing rope is then passed around the back of the bollard and the normal belay taken well below. The trench should be at least a foot deep and the snow in front should be left undisturbed. The anchor may be strengthened by placing ice axes at the back or by padding the rope around the bollard with rucksacks, spare clothes, newspapers, etc.

3. **Ice Axe and Snow Stake Anchors** (Fig.3. page 88).
   The ice axe and snow stake anchors are really suspect and should only be used in iron hard snow when time is pressing. Place it at right angles to the slope and tilt the top back a few degrees from the vertical then hammer home. (If there are spare people available they can stand on the axe head and linked axe belays can be constructed one above the other). Attach a long sling and belay well below this in a sitting position to ensure that the belay rope runs almost parallel to the surface of the snow. Another method of ice axe belay is to cut a large step and hammer the axe in vertically at the back of the step. This is also more effective with a person standing on the axe head. Always use a metal or fibre glass shafted axe for this method of belaying and only use in iron hard snow.

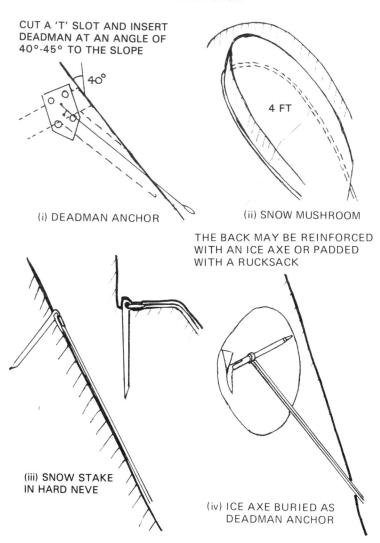

CUT A 'T' SLOT AND INSERT
DEADMAN AT AN ANGLE OF
40°-45° TO THE SLOPE

40°

(i) DEADMAN ANCHOR

4 FT

(ii) SNOW MUSHROOM

THE BACK MAY BE REINFORCED
WITH AN ICE AXE OR PADDED
WITH A RUCKSACK

(iii) SNOW STAKE
IN HARD NEVE

(iv) ICE AXE BURIED AS
DEADMAN ANCHOR

Anchors on Ice

As with snow it is impossible to guarantee really secure belays on ice, however, in emergency they may have to be used.

1. **Ice Bollard**

   In spite of the advances in ice screw design this is still probably the best belay on ice. A bollard is cut out of a solid boss of ice about 18 inches across and 24 inches long. The trench should be 6 inches deep and cut in at the back to hold the rope in position. Any starring or opaqueness in the centre of the bollard is an indication that it is unsound. (Fig. 2. page 90)

2. **Natural Anchors**

   Occasionally, natural ice anchors occur - ice pillars, natural ice pinnacles, edges and flakes of ice which can be cut into anchor points with the ice axe.

3. **Ice Screws**

   There are three basic types of ice pitons.

   i.   The drive-in cut-out old conventional type, which may now be regarded as obsolete.

   ii.   The drive-in screw-release, and

   iii.   The screw-in screw-release.

   There is no ice screw or piton which is the ideal - they each have their advantages and disadvantages and one must use different screws for different types of ice. The Salewa tubular ice screw is suitable for brittle ice as it is hollow and extracts a core of ice as it is screwed in. The Salewa drive-in screw-release ice piton is good for other types of ice although it requires a great deal of effort to hammer into hard ice. The effectiveness of any type of ice screw ultimately depends upon the strength of the ice.

Placement of Ice Screws (page 90)

1. Always put into sound ice; if the surface is brittle or soft cut it away to expose the good ice below. As with a rock peg the head of an ice screw may afford support and it should be inserted with the eye down and the head flush to the ice. When cutting away rotten ice, to insert a drive-in screw-release piton, ensure there is sufficient clearance for the head to rotate for extraction.

2. The angle of insertion is 90 degrees.

3. Starring occurs in brittle ice with most screws although the Salewa tubular is less liable to cause starring than any others.

BELAYING ON ICE

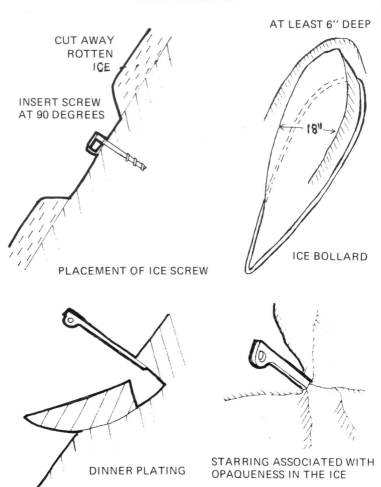

CUT AWAY
ROTTEN
ICE

INSERT SCREW
AT 90 DEGREES

PLACEMENT OF ICE SCREW

AT LEAST 6" DEEP

←18"→

ICE BOLLARD

DINNER PLATING

STARRING ASSOCIATED WITH
OPAQUENESS IN THE ICE

4. **Dinner Plating** - This occurs in brittle ice when the insertion of a piton chisels off large lumps of ice shaped rather like a dinner plate. Care should be taken when inserting an ice piton above head height, as the ice may break away onto the climber.

5. **General** - Always use more than one ice piton for a belay and link in the same way as rock pegs. Never place them too close together and always try to place them in separate ice bosses. Avoid placing an ice piton near the edge of a horizontal step as it may break off the lip of the step. A large step may be cut in easy angled ice and the piton placed near the back of the step in a vertical plane.

Notes on the Placement of Different Screws

Salewa tubular - cut a small hole with the pick of the axe to start the screw. Hammer slightly to start screw whilst screwing it at the same time. Use the pick or shaft of the axe or another screw as a lever in the karabiner eye hole.

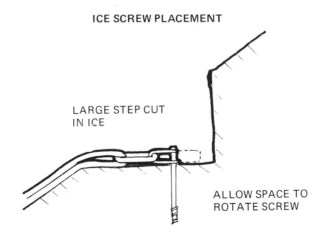

ICE SCREW PLACEMENT

LARGE STEP CUT IN ICE

ALLOW SPACE TO ROTATE SCREW

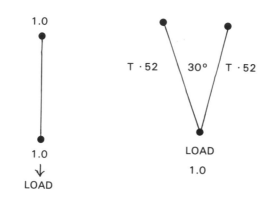

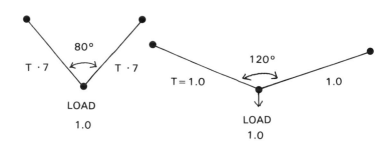

THE LOAD DISTRIBUTION ON SLINGS AT DIFFERENT ANGLES.
LOAD INCREASES AS ANGLE INCREASES

Linking Belays

In rescue situations secure belays are essential and it is sound policy to link belays for safety. All belays should be linked in such a way that the strain acts simultaneously on all the anchor points. In some instances it may be thought necessary to link all main belays with a rope, so each separate system backs up its neighbour. In the diagram (i) position (c) is supported by (a) and (b) and the connection ropes are tensioned so as to give immediate support. The adjusting of slings can be achieved by tying them in sheet bends which are easily adjustable, or by taking a twist of the spare rope around the karabiner. In diagram (ii) the failure of peg (b) will result in a swing and the shock loading of piton (a) which could then fail. The correct way to link pegs (a) and (b) would be to use two slings meeting midway and well below the pitons. Diagram (iii) shows an incorrect way of linking the pegs with separate slings. Again, if either peg fails, the sling will slide through the other and it will be shock loaded with a risk of failure.

All linking of pitons should take into consideration the type of placement of the piton and the direction of pull resulting from the linkage.

LINKING BELAYS

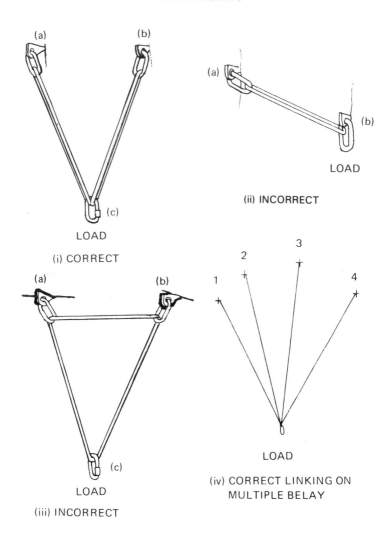

(a)   (b)

(c)

LOAD

(i) CORRECT

(a)   (b)

LOAD

(ii) INCORRECT

(a)   (b)

(c)

LOAD

(iii) INCORRECT

1   2   3   4

LOAD

(iv) CORRECT LINKING ON MULTIPLE BELAY

SELF ADJUSTING BELAYS

(i) TWO POINTS JOINED WITH ONE SLING

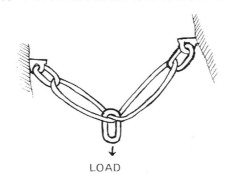

LOAD

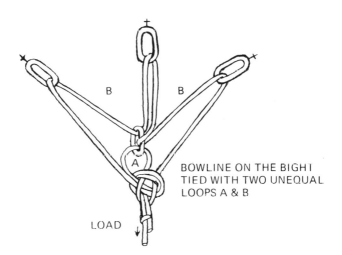

BOWLINE ON THE BIGHT
TIED WITH TWO UNEQUAL
LOOPS A & B

LOAD

(ii) THREE POINTS JOINED IN SELF ADJUSTING SYSTEM

CHAPTER V

ROPE TECHNIQUES

1. Conventional Roped Climbing

In this method one climber is always anchored and belaying his partner thus ensuring a constant safeguard.

2. Moving Together

a. This method has several variations but basically involves both men safeguarding each other whilst climbing together on a short length of rope. With 150′ rope 50′ would be coiled either end and the middle 50′ would be used, some of which would be carried in hand coils. Maximum use would be made of natural spikes and when climbing ridges the two climbers would attempt to stay either side of the ridge which would act as a natural running belay.

b. Moving together on artifical climbs. In some instances e.g. on extended bolt/peg ladders it may be quicker to move together. The climbers use one 150′ rope doubled and climb 75′ apart using another 150′ rope as a continuous loop for hauling up equipment from the second to the leader as the latter exhausts his equipment.

3. Yosemite Method

This method has been developed for climbing long aid climbs. The leader has two ropes - a climbing rope and a sack hauling rope. At the end of each pitch he ties off the climbing rope and rigs a Yosemite Lift on the sack hauling rope to hoist the haul sack. Meanwhile the second man ascends the climbing rope using Jumars. He safeguards himself from a long fall in the event of Jumar slip/ failure by tying into the rope at reasonable intervals using a Figure ot Eight knot on the bight (he is already secured to the end).

4. Self Belaying - Solo Climbing

a. Z system. This involves tying off the end of the climbing rope and taking 20′ and tying on with a Figure of Eight knot on the bight. The climber then ascends placing runners to safeguard himself until he reaches a conventional spot within 20′ where he can tie into a further 20′. He continues this way until he reaches the end of the rope. As an additional safeguard the climber can attach himself to the rope with a prusik although this may not

SYSTEM FOR MOVING TOGETHER

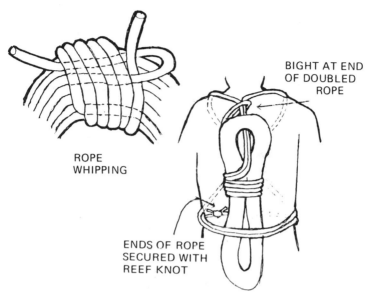

ROPE
WHIPPING

BIGHT AT END
OF DOUBLED
ROPE

ENDS OF ROPE
SECURED WITH
REEF KNOT

COILING A ROPE
DOUBLED FOR CARRYING

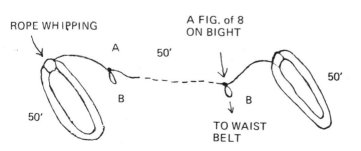

ROPE WHIPPING

A FIG. of 8
ON BIGHT

A

50'

B

50'

50'

B

TO WAIST
BELT

hold a fall it could be used for resting. Next he ties off the climbing rope and secures a second rope he has been trailing and which is also fastened to the lower belay point. He rappels down this second rope and prusiks up the fixed climbing rope removing his protection until he regains the upper belay point.

b.   Short loop system. This method involves climbing on a short continuous loop which is always clipped into three or more pegs. The climber ascends/descends moving up his attachment points from bottom to top. This is less safe than the previous method as he is always relying on only three or four pitons at the same time. A variation of this is to use two or three long slings which are clipped up from lower to higher pegs.

5.   Artifical Climbing

A detailed explanation of artifical or aid climbing is beyond the scope of this book. There are two basic systems of climbing which in part depend whether or not the pitons are in place (a) The Yosemite method which has already been described (b) The classic method where the pegs are generally in situ. The latter method involves conventional roped climbing. Both methods use etrier or stirrups to clip into pitons and bolts. The traditional method of aid climbing used tension i.e. the rope was clipped into the peg above the climber who was held into the rock by tension from the second. This system has in part been supplanted by using a cowstail or short sling which is clipped or hooked (fifi hook) into the piton. Some climbers use a chain of short slings called a daisy chain to allow for adjustment. Other methods of counterbalance include crossing the feet and back stepping both of which allow the climber to hold himself in balance with less expenditure of effort. Yet another method is to sit in etrier up to the thigh - this is useful when negotiating overhangs and roofs.

Aid climbing requires considerable practice and organisation and use of equipment before one becomes fully proficient. Care must be taken to develop the correct sequence of movement and every effort should be made to reduce rope drag by using double rope technique and not slavishly clipping in to every piton. Conservation of energy and efficient use of time are the key to fast aid climbing.

METHODS OF COUNTERBALANCE WHEN AID CLIMBING

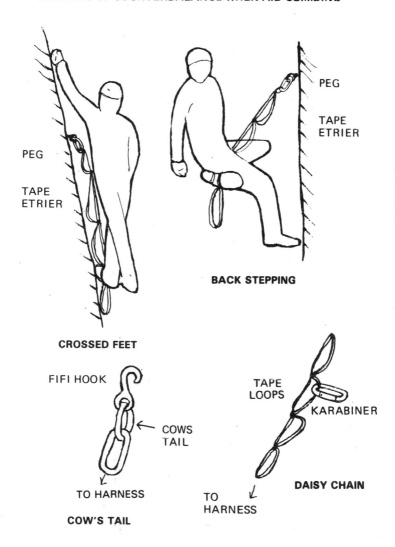

PEG

TAPE ETRIER

CROSSED FEET

PEG

TAPE ETRIER

BACK STEPPING

FIFI HOOK

COWS TAIL

TO HARNESS

COW'S TAIL

TAPE LOOPS

KARABINER

DAISY CHAIN

TO HARNESS

CHAPTER VI
DOUBLE ROPE TECHNIQUE

The double rope technique of climbing is used extensively in Britain and Europe on routes of high technical standard. In its simplest form, it is the use of two belaying ropes instead of one. This chapter explains how the system works and presents some of its advantages and disadvantages.

Ropes

A continuous 300' rope with the centre clearly marked, or two separate lengths of 150' rope are used.

The usual combination is two separate 150' x 9mm ropes, although some climbers prefer the heavier, but much stronger combination of two 150' x 11mm ropes. A useful compromise is one each. By using two spearate ropes, a climbing team has several options available to them. For example, the climber may wish to switch to single rope technique on relatively easy terrain, since management is easier. Also, a team may wish to unrope for easy sections of a climb, in which case each climber would carry a rope, equally sharing the load, and have something to work with in the event of a mishap.

The single 300' long rope has both advantages and disadvantages. It requires careful management and tangles can be difficult to unravel even with bi-coloured ropes. It is easier to manage if coiled into two separate 150' coils rather than one enormous coil. On the other hand, the absence of a connecting knot is an adantage on abseils (rappels). When recovering the rope, it is much less likely to jam in a crack, snag on trees or ledges, or dislodge rocks.

Tying In and Belaying

Each climber ties into both ropes, taking care to keep them separated and running free. If a single, 300' length is used, fewer problems result if the lead climber first ties into the middle and then pays out the rope chasing twists and kinks out the two free ends.

If a karabiner is used to tie-in with a double length rope, remember to tie the Figure of Eight loop in bight of the rope so that it is a double loop. Otherwise the full strength advantage of two ropes is not realized. Similarly, when tying into two separate ropes, two separate karabiners should be used.

When using a double rope system, each rope should be separately belayed to different anchors.

The standard method of belaying in Britain is the waist (hip) belay, which needs no modification for double rope technique. While not all mountaineering texts agree, I recommend that the ropes go around the waist above the line to the anchor instead of below. This insures that the rope is not lost in a severe downward pull. In the event of an upward pull, it is trapped in the armpits, although in an awkward stance, it may be better to run the rope through an additional karabiner clipped into the waist loop. However, to be entirely satisfactory, waist belaying must be done in conjunction with good running belays.

The Sticht belay plate is applicable to two rope techniques and a special model with two 9mm holes, side by side, is manufactured. For large ropes, or a combination, two separate plates are used, preferably using separate belay karabiners. For the Munter or Italian hitch (the 'U.I.A.A. Method'), two separate belay karabiners are also in order.

Basic Rope Management

In its simplest application, the lead climber clips one rope, then the next into alternate protection points. Most climbing situations, however, are more complicated, and the climber and belayer must manage the ropes carefully to reduce rope drag and avoid tangles.

The belayer must insure that the two ropes remain separated and do not twist together, otherwise runners may be lifted from spikes and horns or twists may jam at pegs or nuts.

The leader must also exercise judgement in using running belays. He must avoid zig-zagging the rope by carefully selecting his placements and by the use of slings. The two ropes should never cross each other and should as far as possible follow parallel courses. This may necessitate clipping the same rope into two or more running belays on the left of his route before finding a running belay on his right for the other rope.

If the pitch ends with a long, unprotected run-out, it is best to clip both ropes into the last running belay point. Use separate karabiners for each rope, since two ropes may exert a levering effect on the gate. There is also some danger of the ropes abrading each other in the event of a fall.

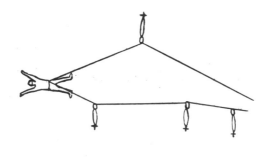

INCORRECT DOUBLE ROPE TECHNIQUE. AVOIDABLE ROPE CRISS-CROSS CAUSES ROPE DRAG.

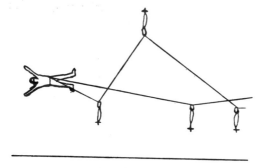

ROPE DRAG ON SINGLE ROPE.

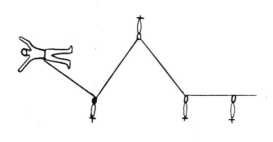

CORRECT DOUBLE ROPE TECHNIQUE. BOTH ROPES FOLLOW NEARLY PARALLEL LINES WITHOUT SHARP BENDS.

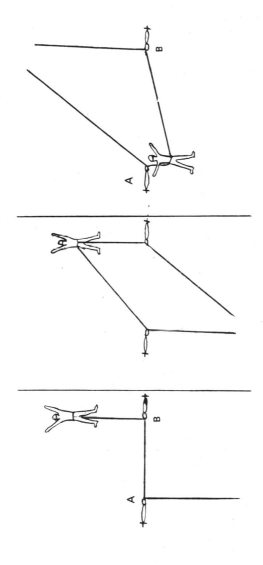

WITH SINGLE ROPE TECHNIQUE THE SECOND CLIMBER IS UNPROTECTED ON THE TRAVERSE FROM A TO B.

CORRECT USE OF DOUBLE ROPE ON THE SAME TRAVERSE.

WITH DOUBLE ROPE, THE SECOND CLIMBER WILL BE WELL PROTECTED DURING THE TRAVERSE FROM A TO B.

103

Traversing Manoeuvres

Two rope technique is especially advantageous on traverses. It allows the leader to fully protect his seond without sacrificing any of his own protection. When the traverse is reached, the leader clips only one rope into the first running belay point. The second rope is clipped into all subsequent belays. After completion of the traverse, the lead climber continues on up and the first rope now provides a nearly overhead belay for the second.

This procedure, of course, is effective only when the traverse is followed by a vertical section of climbing. In pure traverses, and in tension traverses where the climber must take tension on the first running belay, an alternate method is used. Here the second leaves one rope clipped into the first, or tension belay point. This rope is paid out by the belayer while the other is taken in. At the end of the traverse, the second unties from the back rope and it is recovered by pulling it through the tension anchor.

Abseils and Pendulum Manoeuvres

The obvious advantage in an abseil situation is the extra length of rope which allows longer drops between stations. It also makes it possible to belay the first man down a long drop, or to belay both climbers on shorter drops.

The double rope is also useful in pendulum moves, whether they are done on rappel or under tension. One rope is used as the pendulum rope while the other is used to initiate the pendulum. It is also a safeguard, since the leader can be pulled back to the starting position in the event he cannot reach his objective.

Other Considerations

The double rope technique allows many difficult rope manoeuvres to be made with greater safety. One rope is used for the manoeuvre, the other for a back-up belay. For example, one rope may be used for lassoing a spike or rigging a Tyrolean traverse, while the other is used to safeguard a manoeuvre. When prusiking is necessary, you can simultaneously belay against the possibility of knot slippage. On long climbs or awkward pitches, chimneys for example, the second rope can be used to haul a rucksack. In this stuation, the sack should be hauled before the second comes up. In case it hangs up, he is still in a position to climb up and free it.

The double rope system is much stronger than the single rope system and consequently gives greater security to the leader in the event of a fall. There is far less likelihood of two ropes being cut by an edge or severed by stone fall simultaneously. Additionally, the party is not stranded by a damaged rope and they can continue on the other.

Thus it can be seen that double rope technique has many advantages on difficult climbs. Its greatest advantage, however, is the increased security it affords the leader. It doubles his safety factor.

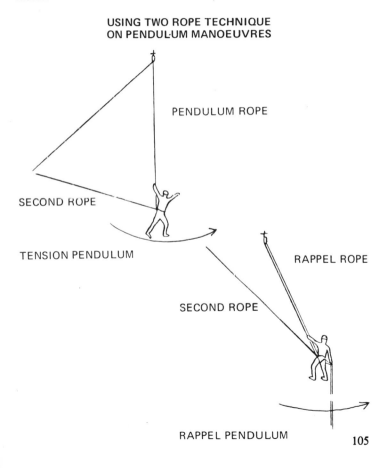

USING TWO ROPE TECHNIQUE
ON PENDULUM MANOEUVRES

PENDULUM ROPE

SECOND ROPE

TENSION PENDULUM

RAPPEL ROPE

SECOND ROPE

RAPPEL PENDULUM

CHAPTER VII

PRUSIK KNOTS AND ASCENDERS

The Prusik Knot is a special knot tied on a climbing rope using 5mm or 7mm cord which jams and holds its position when under load. When it is unloaded it is possible to loosen it and move the sling up or down the rope. This is a fundamental principle in rope rescue and consequently the term has become generic for all jam/release knots and for the action of climbing a rope using this method. Since the invention of the prusik by Dr.Karl Prusik many other knots have been invented at different times in different countries with different names. However, all sliding knots follow the same principle - the winding of a thinner rope around the main climbing rope to provide friction under load - this is then tied off in various ways. They have varying advantages and disadvantages and the choice of knot is left to the individual's personal experience and practice.

The prusik knot has been partially replaced by the development of mechanical ascenders which are easier to use under most circumstances. As with the Prusik the Jumar has become the generic name for the mechanical prusikers and 'Jumaring' is the action of using these pieces of equipment. The principal ascenders are the Jumar (CMI), the Petzl Expedition (Clog), and the Gibbs. A recent development has been the design of ascenders with special functions such as the Shunt which is designed for use on two ropes as a rappel safety device. Although ascenders are superior to prusik knots and karabiner/knot combinations they do have the following disadvantages.

i. They are expensive and it is doubtful that such an investment is necessary unless you are contemplating doing a great deal of prusiking.

ii. Unlike the prusik knots most ascenders cannot be used on doubled ropes, e.g. for safeguarding a person rappelling. The exception noted is the Petzl Shunt.

iii. They are extra items of equipment to carry and have one use as opposed to slings and karabiners which have many.

iv. As mechanical devices they may break or malfunction due to fatigue and wear.

As with the prusik knots the climber should make up his own mind regarding the relative efficiency of the different equipment by personal practice and experiment. Always follow instructions carefully when using mechanical ascenders since they must be operated correctly to obtain the maximum advantage.

THE PRUSIK

The Prusik knot is tied with 5mm, 6mm or 7mm tensile cord on half 9mm or full rope 11mm. The sling is simply wound around the rope and threaded through itself twice, taking care the second winding is within the first. The knot should be kept symmetrical and there should be no overlapping of the windings otherwise it could slip under load. Under certain conditions two wraps may slip and the grip ability of the knot can be improved by adding a third wrap within the knot. When 5mm tensile cord is used it tends to cut into the user and is more susceptible to jamming. Under a shock load a prusik knot tied in 5mm tensile cord may abrade and fuse, and if it is of hawser laid construction, kinks up, knotting the strands. Such a situation developed when a climber rappelling with a 5mm prusik loop attached to the rope as a safeguard, lost control, and descended out of control: he was saved but only just by a prusik. A 7mm prusik is much stronger and safer to use and is less liable to act in this way. The new kevlar tensile cord with a breaking strain of 9mm rope may provide a very strong prusik system if the handling properties of the cord are suitable to knot tying.

The great advantage of the prusik knot is that it is easy to tie and can be attached with one hand. The easiest way to tie the knot is to roll the knot fastening the prusik sling (double fishermans) around the main rope twice and pull it through the sling loop. This may be useful when hanging free on the rope after a fall or tying off the loaded belay rope when your partner has fallen off. The effectiveness of a prusik may vary according to the following:

i. Type of rope - laid or sheath
ii. Type of prusik cord - laid or sheath - perlon or kevlar
iii. Stiffness of the rope
iv. Water content
v. Dirt
vi. Temperature

The importance of practice in safe controlled conditions cannot be over emphasized.

Prusik with Karabiner

The prusik knot may be tied around a karabiner which provides a

SLIDING FRICTION KNOTS

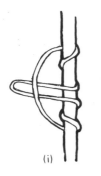  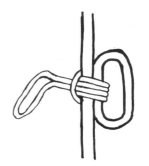

(i) (ii)

PRUSIK KNOT

PRUSIK KNOT TIED WITH
A KARABINER

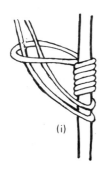  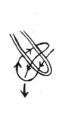

(i) (ii) (iii)

KLEMHEIST KNOT

KLEMHEIST KNOT TIED OFF
WITH A SHEET BEND

SLIDING FRICTION KNOTS

BACHMANN KNOT

KLEMHEIST KNOT TIED
WITH A KARABINER

 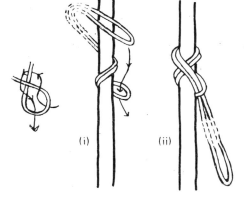

PENBERTHY KNOT
TIED WITH A LENGTH
OF ROPE WHICH IS
THEN JOINED

(i)   (ii)

KREUZKLEM

handhold facilitating the moving of the knot and is less susceptible to jamming. This would work more effeciently with a D shaped karabiner with the vertical stem of the D next to the rope.

The Klemheist Knot

The sling is wound around the main rope in a spiral and then threaded through itself - the amount of friction can be controlled by increasing or decreasing the number of turns. This knot can be tied using 1″ tubular nylon webbing on 11mm rope and it will grip and slide like tensile cord. Another version is tied off with a sheet bend, an improvement added by John Zwangill. Although requiring time and two hands to tie this improved version works very well and is less liable to jam and easier to loosen than the prusik.

Bachmann

In this knot the sling is clipped into a karabiner and wound round the main rope and the back bar of the karabiner in a descending spiral. The friction can be controlled by the number of turns. This is a superior knot to the prusik as it works better on wet and icy ropes, although it has to be tied using two hands. This knot is especially useful in pulley systems used for hoisting casualties.

The Klemheist Knot with Karabiner

This is simply the knot tied around the main rope and the karabiner. It is very effective and easier to release as the karabiner provides a secure handhold.

The Kreuzklem

This is tied in the reverse direction to the Klemheist - the sling is wound around and up the main rope once and threaded back through itself. This is a simple and effective knot which is easily loosened by pushing the end of the looped sling with the thumb.

The Penberthy Knot

The Penberthy knot is tied with a length of rope wound in a spiral around the climbing rope and tied with a bowline which is adjusted so as to tighten the spiral turns of the rope. The two ends of the sling are then joined in the conventional way, i.e., fisherman's or double fisherman's. This is a very effective knot which does not jam, but does take time to tie. A quick improvised method of tying a type of Penberthy knot is to weight a sling with a karabiner and spin this around the rope and thread the sling through the karabiner.

JUMAR ASCENDER

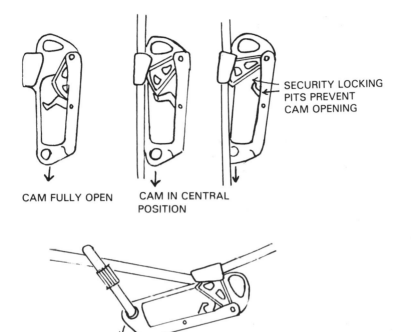

CAM FULLY OPEN CAM IN CENTRAL
POSITION

SECURITY LOCKING
PITS PREVENT
CAM OPENING

DIAGONAL JUMARING
CLIP BOTTOM KRAB INTO ROPE

Jumar Ascender
The original Jumar Clamp has been replaced by a redesigned and
much stronger model removing the faults in the earlier model. The
clamp consists of a rectangular metal handle with a semi circular
sleeve through which the rope runs. The rope is kept in place by a
spring loaded cam of chrome steel with wear resisting teeth which
bite into the rope and hold. When a load is placed on the Jumar the
cam is forced up and into the rope in the sleeve. A spring loaded
safety trigger acting upwards prevents the clamp from opening too
far when being moved up or down the rope.

111

The design improvements include:

i. Larger and stronger handle.
ii. Karabiner eye hole/sling attachment point added to base.
iii. Redesigned sleeve and cam allowing increased contact with rope.
iv. Three positions for safety trigger - closed for safety, control position for moving up rope, fully open holding cam down for placing on and taking off the rope. Some people find these three positions too finicky.

The Jumar works on ropes from 6mm to 14mm diameter and comes in left and right hand models. It weighs 260 grams and is tested to 500 kilograms. It is easily operated with one hand - to place it onto the rope depress the safety trigger with the middle finger and the spring loaded cam with the thumb and clip onto the rope. Sometimes the Jumar may jam on descent and the cam cannot be depressed - in this instance push the clamp up a little to release the spring. When using jumars avoid an overlap as they may jam as one is forced at an angle to the rope. Under cold icy conditions the teeth on the cam may become filled with ice and may slip on an icy rope. In this situation clean the teeth with a sharp instrument. When using Jumars on a diagonal fixed rope, it is necessary to clip the karabiner onto the bottom eye hole into the rope. This prevents loading the jumar at an unsafe angle which may cause it to twist off the rope.

The Petzl Expedition Ascender/Jammer
Both these ascenders work on the spring cam principle similar to the jumar but has double action on the cams which allow them to be locked open by latching on the outside of the handle. When the ascender is on the rope the cam is prevented from opening by a catch which acts as a safety trigger. They are made of sheet metal and have a load bearing capacity of 400kg. The expedition model has a large comfortable hand, with an insulated plastic grip giving plenty of room for large mitts. The cam can be opened by a simple thumb movement on the catch knob which comes in two sizes - short for caving use and long for expedition use when thick mitts are worn. The ascender weighs 195g and comes in left and right hand models.

Other Ascenders of Similar Design
Clog and Kong manufacture similar ascenders to the Petzl expedition model. The Kong weighs 235g and has a breaking load of 650kg. It has a modified version with a built in pulley attachment to the lower part of the handle to facilitate its use in rescue hoisting.

PETZL ASCENDERS

EXPEDITION
ASCENDER

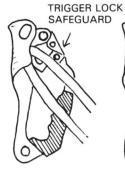

TRIGGER LOCK
SAFEGUARD

ROPE LOCK
OPERATING

FULLY COCKED
OPEN

JAMMER EXPEDITION
ASCENDER MINUS HANDLE

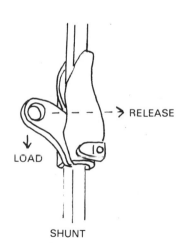

RELEASE

LOAD

SHUNT

The Jammer
The Jammer is really an expedition ascender with the handle removed and is consequently smaller, lighter 135g and less expensive.

The Shunt
The Shunt is primarily designed as a safety device when rappelling and operates on a different principle from the Expedition and the Jammer. A lever system is used to provide graduated braking avoiding shock loads. The rope is gripped by smooth surfaces and can be released under load by pulling down on the body of the device. When the body of the device is released the load of the climber is transferred to the levered cam and the braking is effected. To continue the rappel the climber pulls down once more on the body of the Shunt. The Shunt can be used on single or doubled ropes if the same size from 5 to 12mm in diameter and is said to hold well on icy ropes.

The Gibbs Ascender
The Gibbs Ascender consists of a cam, cam housing or sleeve, and a quick release pin, the cam teeth and smooth rounded parallel bars. The device completely encircles the rope with the quick release pin passing through both sides of the cam housing so that the ascender cannot come off the rope accidentally. This makes the ascender very safe to use but in order to bypass an anchor point on a fixed line it is necessary to remove and separate the parts to disengage it from the rope. All parts are attached to the cam housing or sleeve by small chain links so they cannot be dropped or lost when disengaged. The cam is also spring loaded which is tensioned by clipping the end of the spring onto a lap on the lower part of the cam housing. The Gibbs holds very well on wet, muddy and icy ropes and unlike other ascenders is not prone to ice build up. For this reason it is very good for crevasse rescue. The device is tested to 454 kilograms load.

GIBBS ASCENDER

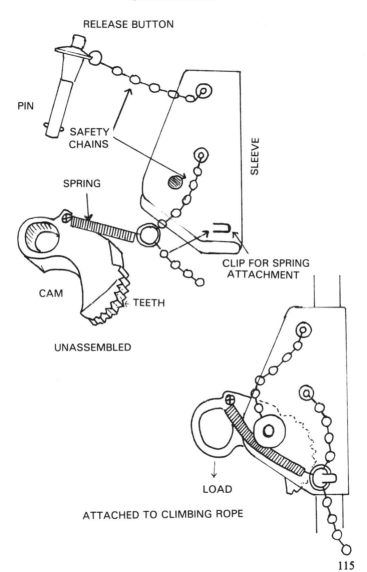

RELEASE BUTTON

PIN

SAFETY CHAINS

SPRING

CAM

TEETH

SLEEVE

CLIP FOR SPRING ATTACHMENT

UNASSEMBLED

LOAD

ATTACHED TO CLIMBING ROPE

115

CHAPTER VIII
HOISTING

There is little doubt that of all the improvised rescue techniques hoisting is one of the most serious to undertake. The following disadvantages should be noted.

i. Considerable strain is placed on anchors - secure anchors are essential.
ii. Considerable wear and tear on equipment especially on ropes running over edges.
iii. Strenuous.
iv. Technical and often complicated.
v. Requires skilled competent personnel to operate effectively and trouble shoot malfunctions.

Whenever possible hoisting should be avoided and some other technique employed, e.g. lowering to the bottom or traversing off. The degree of difficulty experienced depends upon the number of people available, the equipment available and most important of all the ability of the victim to assist himself. The situation may be classified as follows:

a. Self Hoist - using prusik slings or ascenders a person can climb up a rope. There is a wide range of different methods operating on the same principles.
b. Assisted Hoist - where assistance is given from above as well as self help from the victim, e.g. Bilgiri Method, Two-in-One Karabiner Hoist.
c. Unassisted Hoist - where all the work is done at the top by the rescuers. This the most strenous of the hoists. The Yosemite lift and the Z pulley hoists are examples of the fully assisted hoist.

Further Considerations on Hoisting
The setting up of an efficient hoisting system depends upon reducing unnecessary friction on the rescue rope and utilizing the maximum mechanical advantage. This is achieved by (a) management of rope running over edges, (b) use of pulley systems, (c) use of pulley blocks.

(a) **Management**
   Management of rope running over edges. All types of hoisting place strain on the rope and abrasion will occur when the rope is

running over rough rock edges under load. Even when climbing a fixed rope the elasticity can result in considerable abrasion at the contact point with the rock. Always try to avoid the rope running over sharp edges at acute angles - high anchor points and narrow ledges can help in these instances. If these are not available pad the edge with spare clothing or a rucksack. In some instances a karabiner or pulley can be rigged to guide the rope away from a rough edge.

(b) **Pulley System**

The pulley system is basically a device for producing a large force from a small force. The pulleys will lose energy not only through friction but because the pulley block attached to the load has to be lifted. It is important therefore the pulley blocks be efficient and light. When the pulley is attached to the anchor there is no advantage and the ratio of load to effort is 1:1. When the pulley is attached to the load and one end of the rope anchored alone passed through the pulley and hauled up the ratio of load to effort becomes 2:1. A simple formula to obtain the load to effort ratio is to count the number of ropes holding the load. A 3:1 ratio is attained by attaching a pulley at the anchor and passing the load rope through and back through a second pulley which is attached to the load rope by a prusik. When the 2:1 and 3:1 systems are combined the ratio of load to effort becomes 6:1. All of the above figures assume frictionless pulleys.

(c) **Pulley Block**

An efficient durable pulley is essential for rescue hoisting since they will greatly reduce the friction of the rope running around karabiners. Pulleys should be designed to give the rope sufficent clearance even if subject to twisting otherwise the sides of the pulley can jam the rope. The best pulleys have self lubricating ball bearings and are more efficient than nylon shear pulleys but more expensive and heavier. Efficiency is measured by dividing the load by the force necessary to raise it through the pulley.

Pulley Efficiency on 11mm Rope

Karabiner	0.60
Salewa Nylon Pulley	0.88
Russ Anderson	0.93
Ball Bearing	

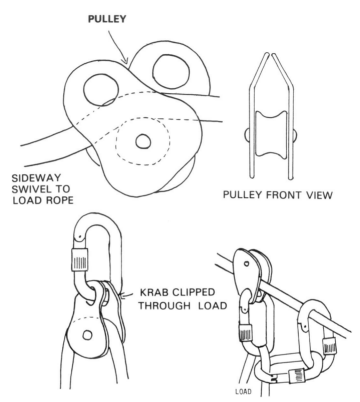

PULLEY

SIDEWAY
SWIVEL TO
LOAD ROPE

PULLEY FRONT VIEW

KRAB CLIPPED
THROUGH LOAD

LOAD

PULLEY TRAMWAY - BACKED UP WITH
TWO ADDITIONAL KARABINERS

TWO METHODS OF SECURING FOOT LOOP

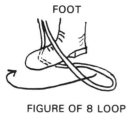

FOOT

FIGURE OF 8 LOOP

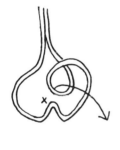

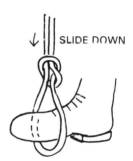

SLIDE DOWN

SLIP KNOT FOR CINCHING FOOT LOOP

(a) **Self-Hoist**

Methods of easing the strain on the waistline when hanging free.

The first essential if one is not wearing some kind of seat or harness is to take weight of the waistline off the chest. This may be accomplished in a variety of ways:

i.   Clip a sling, which is slightly shorter than the waist to foot distance, into the waistline karabiner and stand on it. This immediately takes some of the weight off the waist. The length of the sling is critical and should be determined by practice in a safe situation. In an emergency, a long sling can be shortened by knotting, or several short slings can be joined together.

ii. Tie onto the rope four feet or more from the end and tie a foot loop into the free end of the rope. This can be tucked away until it is required.

iii. Fasten a prusik sling to the rope whenever you think you are in a situation that merits this precaution. The sling is passed through the waistline and tucked away in a pocket. This is the conventional method and when crossing crevassed areas the climber generally attaches two or three prusiks to his climbing rope. Once he has taken the weight off his waist he is in a position to ascend the rope using his prusik slings.

iv. An ingenious method of making a quick improvised seat has been developed by Australian rock climbers and is known as the 'Baboon Hang'. The climber turns upside down to take the weight off the chest and holds this position by trapping a leg behind the climbing rope. A short sling is put over both legs and pulled up to the buttocks. The length of this sling is important and it should be worked out beforehand, although an adjustable sling could be used e.g. tied with a sheet bend. A long sling could be knotted to the required length by tying an overhand. The climber then sits upright by pulling up on the rope; he is now in a ready made seat with a leg loop held either side of the climbing rope.

Once the initial strain is taken off the waist by one of the methods outlined above the climber can prepare his method of ascending the rope in relative comfort.

METHODS OF EASING THE STRAIN ON THE WAIST
WHEN HANGING FREE

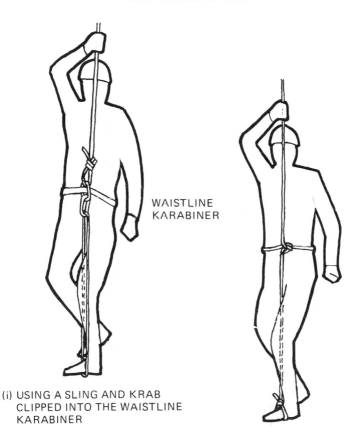

WAISTLINE
KARABINER

(i) USING A SLING AND KRAB
CLIPPED INTO THE WAISTLINE
KARABINER

(ii) TYING ON, LEAVING ENOUGH
ROPE SPARE FOR A FOOT LOOP

METHODS OF EASING THE STRAIN ON THE WAISTLINE WHEN HANGING FREE

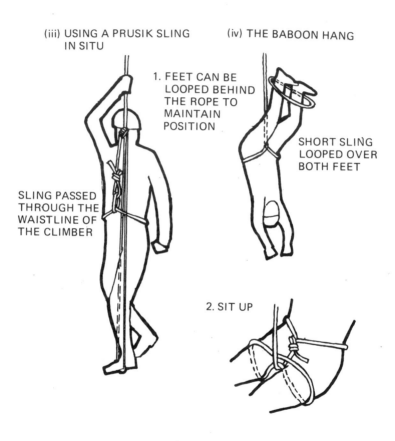

(iii) USING A PRUSIK SLING IN SITU

(iv) THE BABOON HANG

1. FEET CAN BE LOOPED BEHIND THE ROPE TO MAINTAIN POSITION

SHORT SLING LOOPED OVER BOTH FEET

SLING PASSED THROUGH THE WAISTLINE OF THE CLIMBER

2. SIT UP

Prusiking with two slings.

It is possible to prusik with two long slings passed through the waist line or, better still, a chest harness which is attached to the feet with a larks foot. The climber is held upright and into the rope by either loop when it is held under tension. The climber transfers his weight alternately from one to the other moving up the unloaded sling each time and then stepping up. If the prusik loops are attached to the climbing rope below the level of the chest the chest harness can be clipped to the prusiking rope with a karabiner keeping the climber close to the rope which is always under tension.

Another method, which is probably more comfortable, is to prusik with a sit sling and foot loop. The sit sling is attached to a short prusik and the foot loop is long if it is fastened to the rope above the sit sling prusik Fig.(ii) and short if it is fastened below Fig.(i). The climber sits, unweights the foot loop and moves it up the rope; he then steps up unweights the sit sling prusik which is moved up the rope to a higer position. This method has the advantage of leaving the climber in a comparatively comfortable resting position in a sit sling with a free leg to push off against the cliff face.

The disadvantage of the sit sling method is the tendency to turn upside down as the centre of gravity is above the attachment point. This is especially noticeable on a free prusik where there is no cliff face to prop the leg; or where a load may be carried on the back. The load could be carried slung on a rope from the waist below the centre of gravity, thus increasing stability. A combined chest harness/sit sling could be used thus raising the attachment point above the centre of gravity. This is possibly the most comfortable method of prusiking. Additional security may be provided by securing a short sling from the foot loop prusik to the chest harness, thus safeguarding the climber in the event of failure of his chest prusik. This is particularly advisable when using mechanical prusikers. A further precaution when using mechanical prusikers is to fasten a safety prusik loop above the ascender and attach it to the chest.

There are other combinations and methods of prusiking with which the climber can experiment, adapting the most satisfactory method for his own use.

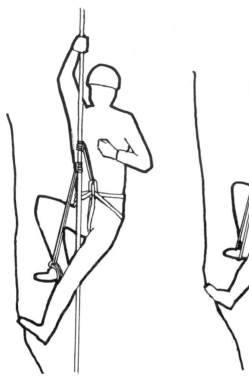

(i) SIT SLING PRUSIK ABOVE
SHORT FOOT LOOP PRUSIK

(ii) SIT SLING PRUSIK BELOW
LONG FOOT LOOP PRUSIK

ASCENDING THE ROPE WITH ONLY ONE PRUSIK

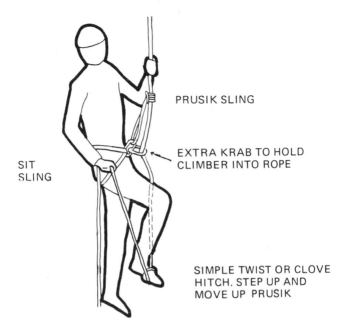

PRUSIK SLING

EXTRA KRAB TO HOLD CLIMBER INTO ROPE

SIT SLING

SIMPLE TWIST OR CLOVE HITCH. STEP UP AND MOVE UP PRUSIK

THE ANKLE HITCH — A METHOD OF SECURING A FOOT LOOP TO THE ANKLE. THIS REQUIRES MORE ROPE BUT IS MORE SECURE THAN A LARKS FOOT

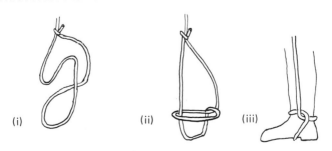

(i)   (ii)   (iii)

Prusiking with three slings

The classic method of climbing a rope is to utilise three prusik loops, one for each foot and one for the chest. The foot loops may be tied off with a larks foot to prevent them falling off the feet when not under tension. The chest loops may be clipped into the waistline karabiner which is moved to the back for this purpose, or it may be tied off at the chest in an overhand knot for additional security. The climber moves one prusik loop at a time and should develop a rhythm especially with the chest prusik of moving up and pushing the prusik up at the same time. Always ensure the load is released before attempting to move the prusik loop up. The length of the prusik loops is important. The chest loop should be shorter than the foot loop. Since individuals vary in size and proportion it would be advisable to experiment in a controlled situation to discover the optimum length of slings. Slings tied with the sheet bend can easily be adjusted in length or they may be shortened by tying overhand or figure of eight knots. Short slings may be lengthened by looping two or three together. The facility for making do with the equipment available is really the crux of improvisation in rescue.

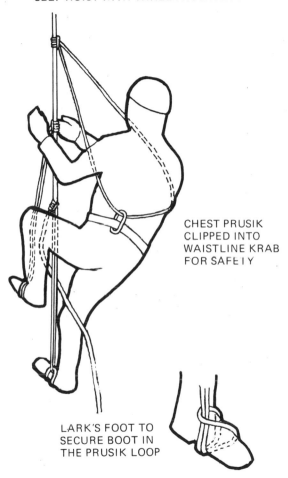

CHEST PRUSIK
CLIPPED INTO
WAISTLINE KRAB
FOR SAFETY

LARK'S FOOT TO
SECURE BOOT IN
THE PRUSIK LOOP

(b) **Assisted Hoists**

In certain situations it is possible for the people above to give assistance to the person below.

i. **Straight Hoist**

On some occasions over a short distance it is possible to pull a person up using a locking prusik and a shoulder belay. A prusik is attached to the climbing rope just below the belayer's waist and the shoulder belay position is adopted with the load rope under the arm and over the opposite shoulder. To lift, bend the knees take in the rope tight and straighten the legs using the powerful leg muscles to lift the casualty. As the rope is hoisted slide the prusik forward to take the load and repeat. This is a strenuous method and can only be used with strong hoisters and light casualties and where the casualty can assist by using holds on the rock face.

ii. **Assisted Stirrup Hoist**

In this method two ropes with sliding foot loops are dropped to the casualty who passes them through his chest harness and around the inside of his thighs to fasten them to the feet. Both ropes are passed through prusik knots at the top. The casualty alternately shifts his weight from one foot to the other thus unloading a rope which can be pulled up through the prusik the distance of a high step. On stepping up the other rope is unloaded and the operation repeated. Clear communication between the casualty and hoister is essential for a smooth hoist. A similar operation may be performed with the casualty standing in a prusik loop attached to his climbing rope with a foot loop rope lowered to him. In a crevasse rescue situation the second foot loop rope could be the other end of his climbing rope. If the casualty had an injured ankle but was otherwise alright a method using a sit-sling and foot loop could be employed with the casualty using his good leg to step up and the sit-sling as a resting stage.

(ii) ASSISTED STIRRUP HOIST

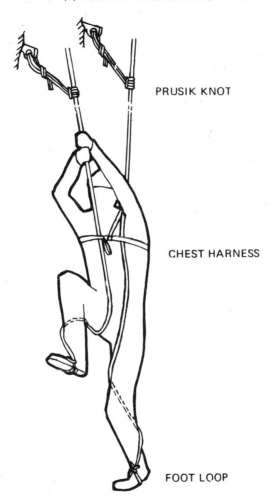

PRUSIK KNOT

CHEST HARNESS

FOOT LOOP

iii. Two in One Karabiner Hoist with Casualty Assisting

This method of hoisting is quite simple and requires little extra equipment. The top man of a pair of roped climbers clips the climbing rope through an anchored karabiner and drops a loop of the rope with a sit-sling and karabiner attached to the lower man. The lower man puts on the sit-sling and clips the karabiner through the loop of rope which now forms an 'S' from himself, up to the anchored krab pulley, down to his sit-sling and finally up to the top man. This end of the rope may be locked off on a prusik fastened to a piton. The top man hoists using a shoulder belay, straight back and bent legs pushing the prusik forward as he lifts to lock off the rope. The lower man can pull on the rope running down to his sit-sling karabiner to assist the hoist. It is possible, however, for the top man to hoist without using assistance from the lower man apart from walking up the face.

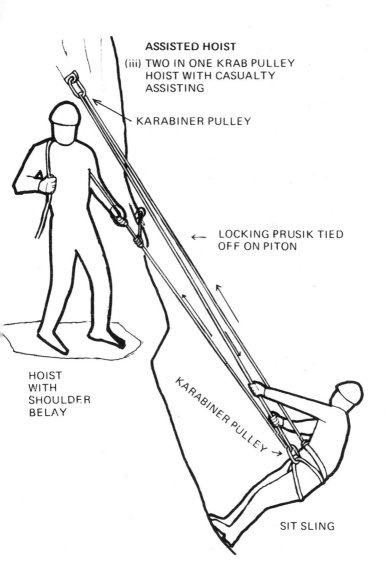

ASSISTED HOIST

(iii) TWO IN ONE KRAB PULLEY
HOIST WITH CASUALTY
ASSISTING

KARABINER PULLEY

LOCKING PRUSIK TIED
OFF ON PITON

HOIST
WITH
SHOULDER
BELAY

KARABINER PULLEY →

SIT SLING

(c) **Unassisted Hoist**
   i) **Yosemite Lift -**
   The Yosemite Lift is a method where the hoister uses his own
   body weight to assist in the operation. The load rope is passed
   through an anchored karabiner pulley and an anchored inverted
   jumar ascender weighted with a gear sling is attached to the
   loaded side. On the other side of the pulley a second jumar
   ascender is attached to the rope and fastened onto the climbing
   harness of the hoister. The load is lifted by the hoister using his
   whole body as a counter weight bending his knees and pulling up
   on the load rope. After each fetch the jumar can be moved up
   the rope to its original height and the action repeated. The
   inverted jumar prevents the rope from sliding back. It is
   important to hoist in the same line as the load rope to ensure
   maximum mechanical advantage.

   An improvement of the Yosemite Lift is shown on the right
   hand side of p.133. In this system the rope is taken through the
   pulley and attached to the second jumar which is also inverted
   and anchored. A karabiner is attached to the loop of rope
   between the jumar and the pulley block and fastened to the
   hoister's harness. The body is once more used as a counter
   weight and the rope pulled up through the second jumar after
   every fetch. This gives a mechanical advantage of 2:1.

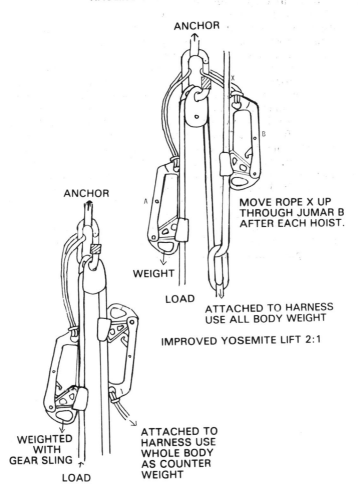

ANCHOR

MOVE ROPE X UP
THROUGH JUMAR B
AFTER EACH HOIST.

WEIGHT

LOAD

ATTACHED TO HARNESS
USE ALL BODY WEIGHT

IMPROVED YOSEMITE LIFT 2:1

ANCHOR

WEIGHTED
WITH
GEAR SLING

LOAD

ATTACHED TO
HARNESS USE
WHOLE BODY
AS COUNTER
WEIGHT

YOSEMITE LIFT 1:1

(ii) **Two in One Bachmann Hoist**

This method makes use of a one way clutch arrangement using a Bachmann knot. The rope is passed through an anchored karabiner which acts as a pulley, and an inverted Bachmann knot is fastened on the load rope side and tied off to a separate anchor point close by. A short prusik loop is then attached to the load rope and the free rope is clipped to it with a karabiner. When the free rope is pulled the Bachmann is jammed against the top pulley karabiner and the rope runs free pulling the bottom prusik up towards the rope anchor. On releasing the free rope the Bachmann comes under tension and locks off the load rope allowing the prusik knot to be slid forward down the load rope in preparation for another hoist. The Bachmann must be anchored close to the pulley karabiner to avoid excessive play on the transfer of load from the pulley karabiner to the Bachmann. It may help if there are two pulley karabiners together giving a longer circumference; they should if possible be smaller than the karabiner on which the Bachmann knot is tied. The further forward the bottom prusik can be pushed the better, as it gives a longer pull with sustained momentum.

(ii) THE TWO IN ONE BACHMANN HOIST

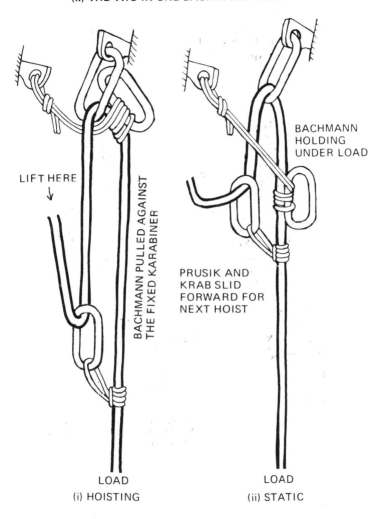

LIFT HERE

BACHMANN PULLED AGAINST THE FIXED KARABINER

BACHMANN HOLDING UNDER LOAD

PRUSIK AND KRAB SLID FORWARD FOR NEXT HOIST

LOAD
(i) HOISTING

LOAD
(ii) STATIC

ONE WAY HOIST SYSTEM

3:1 PULLEY WITH STUFFLESSER HITCH

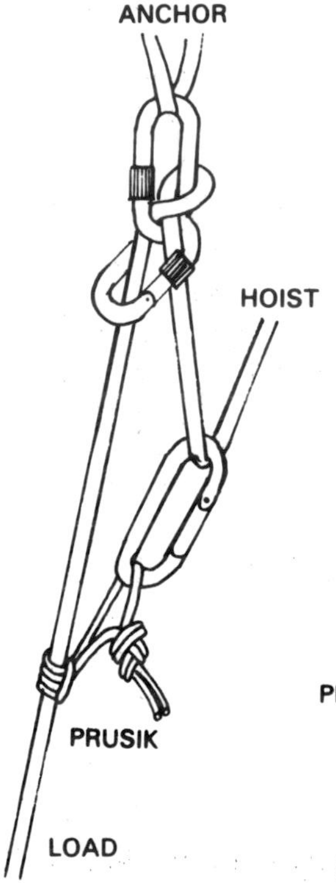

ANCHOR

HOIST

PRUSIK

LOAD

3:1 PULLEY WITH GARDA KNOT

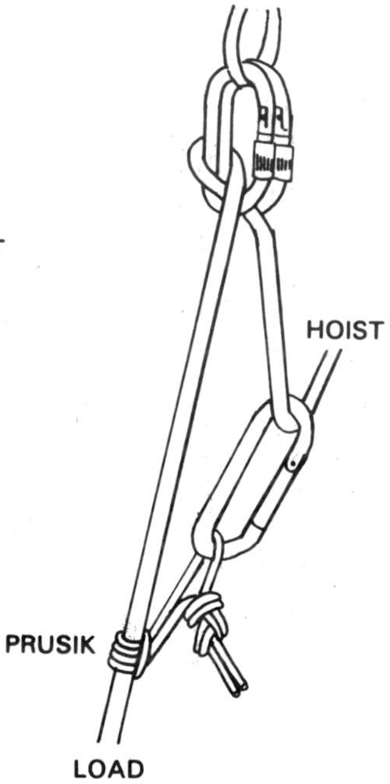

HOIST

PRUSIK

LOAD

N.B.
LOAD AND HOIST ROPES SHOULD NOT BE CONFUSED WHEN USING THIS KNOT.

THE GARDA KNOT — A ONE WAY SYSTEM

ANCHOR

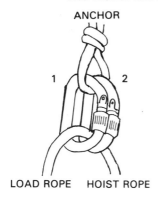

LOAD ROPE   HOIST ROPE

1. CLIP ROPE THROUGH TWO **D** KARABINERS

ANCHOR

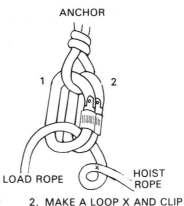

LOAD ROPE

HOIST ROPE

2. MAKE A LOOP X AND CLIP INTO KARABINER 1

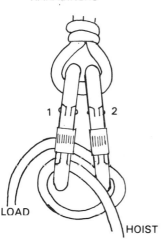

LOAD

HOIST

3. WHEN HOIST ROPE IS PULLED, ROPE RUNS FREELY WITH FRICTION.

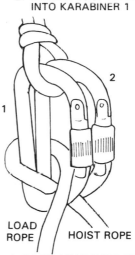

LOAD ROPE   HOIST ROPE

4. WHEN LOAD ROPE IS PULLED, HOIST ROPE IS PINNED BETWEEN TWO KRABS WHICH ARE PULLED TOGETHER

137

THE STUFLESSER HITCH — A ONE WAY SYSTEM

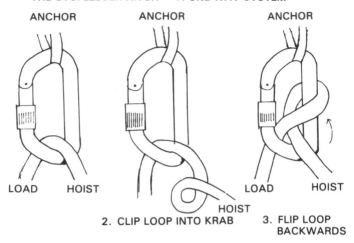

ANCHOR

ANCHOR

ANCHOR

LOAD   HOIST

HOIST

2. CLIP LOOP INTO KRAB

LOAD   HOIST

3. FLIP LOOP BACKWARDS

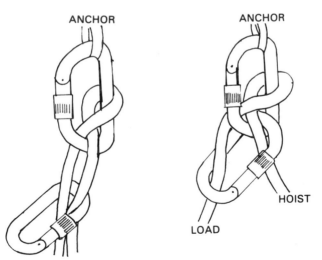

ANCHOR

ANCHOR

HOIST

LOAD

4. CLIP IN KRAB TO BOTH ROPES

5. CLIP SECOND KRAB INTO FIRST KRAB.

IMPROVISED PULLEY SYSTEM USING TRUCKERS HITCH

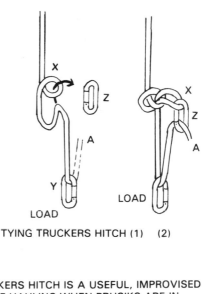

FIG. OF 8

X
Z

A

Y

LOAD

X
Z
A

LOAD

TYING TRUCKERS HITCH (1) (2)

TRUCKERS HITCH

Z

THE TRUCKERS HITCH IS A USEFUL, IMPROVISED
SYSTEM OF HAULING WHEN PRUSIKS ARE IN
SHORT SUPPLY. AT THE END OF EACH HAUL/
FETCH, IT CAN BE UNTIED AND ANOTHER
HITCH RETIED UP AT THE FIG. OF 8.
THE LOAD MUST BE HELD BY LOCKING OFF
THE FIGURE OF 8.

FINAL
POSITION
OF HITCH
ON
COMPLETION
OF ONE
FETCH
OF HAUL

Y

PRUSIK

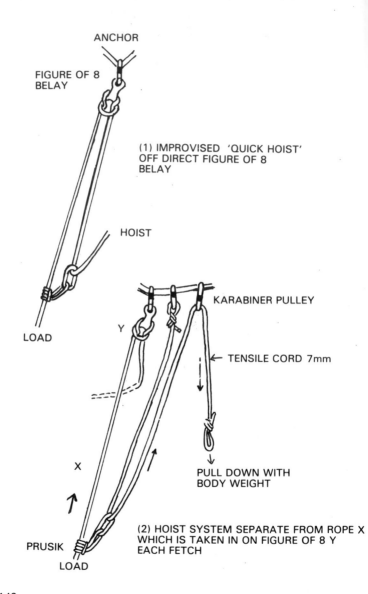

ANCHOR

FIGURE OF 8
BELAY

(1) IMPROVISED 'QUICK HOIST'
OFF DIRECT FIGURE OF 8
BELAY

HOIST

LOAD

KARABINER PULLEY

Y

← TENSILE CORD 7mm

X

PULL DOWN WITH
BODY WEIGHT

PRUSIK

LOAD

(2) HOIST SYSTEM SEPARATE FROM ROPE X
WHICH IS TAKEN IN ON FIGURE OF 8 Y
EACH FETCH

140

KARABINER PULLEY HOIST

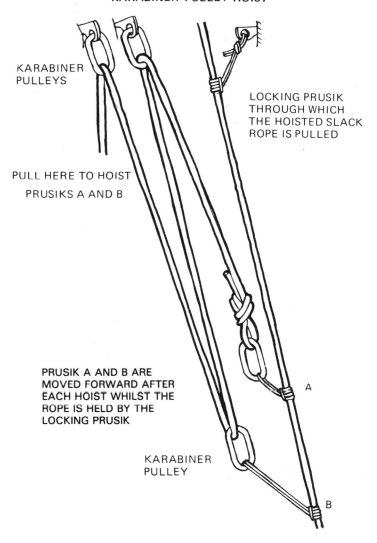

KARABINER PULLEYS

PULL HERE TO HOIST PRUSIKS A AND B

LOCKING PRUSIK THROUGH WHICH THE HOISTED SLACK ROPE IS PULLED

PRUSIK A AND B ARE MOVED FORWARD AFTER EACH HOIST WHILST THE ROPE IS HELD BY THE LOCKING PRUSIK

KARABINER PULLEY

A

B

Rescue of an Unconscious Person Hanging Free on a Waistline Attachment

This situation is a serious one as there is little time in which to carry out the rescue before the person dies from the constricting effect on the rope on the chest. The major difficulty is very often in reaching the person to administer assistance. One method would be to attach an inverted jumar or inverted Bachmann knot to the rope and weight it with a rucksack or some pitons. Attach a back rope to the loaded jumar and allow it to slide down the rope to the hanging climber. The jumar holds under load and the climber can be pulled into the side.

It is essential to take the weight of the climber off his waistline and to transfer it to a sit-sling or chest harness. To accomplish this attach a short prusik loop to the rope above the hanging climber and clip a karabiner into this to act as a pulley. Place the unconscious climber in a sit-sling and attach it to a long sling which is passed through the pulley karabiner and attached to an etrier lifting the hanging climber up into the sit-sling and releasing the weight on the waistline. The sit-sling is then clipped to another prusik attached to the load rope. A chest harness may be attached in the same way.

A METHOD OF EASING THE STRAIN ON A PERSON HANGING UNCONSCIOUS FROM A WAIST LINE ATTACHMENT

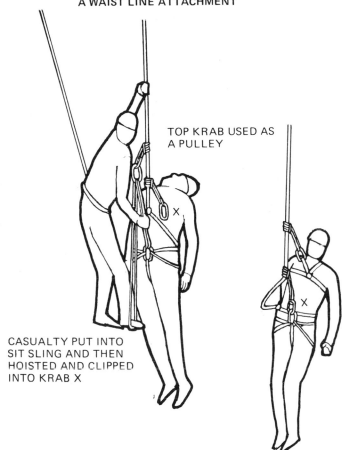

TOP KRAB USED AS A PULLEY

CASUALTY PUT INTO SIT SLING AND THEN HOISTED AND CLIPPED INTO KRAB X

PRUSIK ATTACHED TO CHEST FOR SUPPORT

Tying Off a Belay Rope Under Load

In the event of a fall in which there are no runners or the runners fail, the climber could face a situation where he needs to tie off the belay rope whilst it is directly under load. How this is done depends upon the type of belay system used, the harness and the mode of attachment of the climber to the belay system.

i.   Waist belay/Climbing belt/Belay attachment to waist karabiner clipped into climbing belt ring.

First wrap the inactive rope around the leg and stand on the end. This secures the rope and releases both hands. Then attach a prusik loop to the live rope and clip it back into the karabiner of the belay sling. The prusik is pushed forward and the inactive rope released to transfer the weight to the prusik. The inactive rope is then tied in a figure of 8 knot on the bight and clipped into the belay karabiner. The climber can now undo his swami belt, or climbing belt and release himself from the belay. He is now free to render assistance or to go for help.

This is the quickest method, however, it leaves a static system tied off. It may be better to:

a.   Tie off the prusik in an Italian hitch locked with an overhand slip knot *which can be released under load* (see p.57).

b.   Tie off the main rope in the same manner. This allows a completely mobile system and avoids cutting the prusik.

Further Points

1.   It is considerably easier to tie off a *direct* belay than an indirect belay because the climber is removed from the system.

2.   Where the rope fastens the climbing harness a system of belay attachment should be used that allows the climber to release himself from the system, e.g. if a belay plate is used it should not be attached to the end tie-in loop as a loaded rope would lock the climber into the system.

TYING OFF A BELAY ROPE UNDER LOAD

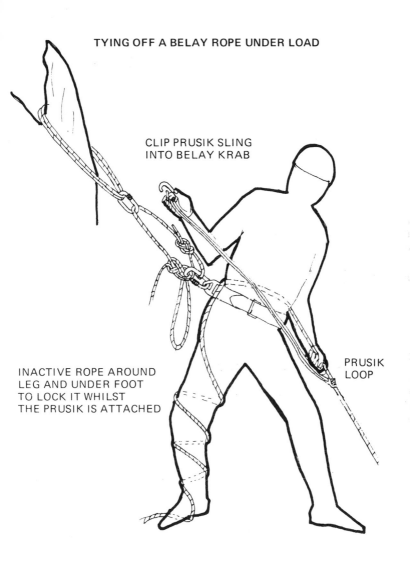

CLIP PRUSIK SLING
INTO BELAY KRAB

INACTIVE ROPE AROUND
LEG AND UNDER FOOT
TO LOCK IT WHILST
THE PRUSIK IS ATTACHED

PRUSIK
LOOP

CHAPTER IX
KARABINER BRAKES

The Karabiner brake is a very useful improvised device wherever any lowering or rappelling is needed. There are many friction devices or descenders on the market, but they are specialized equipment and are carried by few, whereas karabiners are multi-purpose and are carried by many.

To assemble the brake, one karabiner is clipped across the other with the rope running through and over the transverse bar. Once learnt, it is simple to use and saves wear and tear on clothing and expenditure of energy. The brake operated correctly gives a smooth lower, superior to the waist belay lowers. Its applications are many, especially on cliff rescue, e.g. the lowering of stretchers, tragsitz, oneself with a casualty, people who will not, or cannot, abseil and also, or course, abseiling.

As a method of rappelling it has much to recommend it; control and locking are simple and there is no strain on the body. The karabiner brake moves down the rope, consequently it must be inverted in order that the control rope is fed from below. The control rope is held on the back bar side of the karabiner running parallel to the rope, and is passed under the thigh and held on the right hand. If the person wishes to stop, the rope may be wrapped around the thigh, thus locking the brake. This leaves the hands free to deal with emergency situations, e.g. freeing jammed ropes, untangling kinks, administering aid to a person on a cliff, undertaking a difficult pendulum, removing gear, etc.

Assembled Karabiner Brake
1. The load rope is nearest you when facing the brake.
2. The gate of the 1st karabiner points in an anti-clockwise direction.
3. The rope tightens both screw gates as it passes.
4. The control rope is held on the back bar side of the first karabiner, i.e. the karabiner parallel with the rope.
5. The gate of the first karabiner points to the belay. If these are correct, the brake is correct.

ASSEMBLY OF KARABINER BRAKE
WITH CONTROL ROPE BELOW

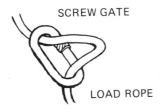

SCREW GATE

LOAD ROPE

(i) HOLD THE KRAB IN RIGHT HAND
WITH THE GATE POINTING UP
AND ANTI CLOCKWISE. PUSH A
LOOP OF ROPE UP FROM BELOW
THROUGH THE KRAB. KEEP THE
LOAD ROPE NEAREST YOU.

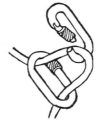

(ii) HOLD THE SECOND KRAB
WITH YOUR LEFT HAND IN
THE SAME POSITION AS THE
FIRST AND CLIP INTO THE
LOOP OF ROPE FROM ABOVE.

(iii) TURN THE SECOND KRAB
GATE UPPERMOST.

(iv) TWIST THE SECOND
KRAB BACK DROPPING
ITS GATE BEHIND
THE FIRST KRAB.

147

Operation of Karabiner Brakes

1.   A fast lower may result in over heating of the karabiner due to friction; the lower should be steady and smooth with a double brake fitted if the load is heavy.

2.   Check the rope for kinks or knots as these could jam the brake. The rope should be fed into the brake to avoid this happening. If there is no danger of the rope snagging it may be left hanging over the cliff.

3.   Remember the brake is a one way system; it cannot reverse without releasing the load and feeding back the rope by hand.

4.   The belay is directly loaded, therefore, reduce the shock loading and the vibration by attaching the karabiner brake with a sling. Always have a karabiner clipped on the belay side of the brake separating it from the sling.

5.   The load on the brake should be constant as jerking and unloading could result in the braking karabiner (transverse to the rope) slipping down and fouling the brake.

6.   It is possible to increase friction and stop the lower by bringing the control rope forward across the brake. A prusik knot may be tied below the brake on the load rope to give an independent locking system. The other end of the prusik sling should be secured by a knot which can be released under tension e.g. Mariner Knot.

7.   When possible the brake operator should feed the rope from a waist belay and should be belayed separately. It is possible, however, to feed hand over hand or even one handed, and with practice one man can operate two brakes. Gloves should be worn.

8.   A brake may be locked and tied off with a bight of rope in a half hitch which can be released under load by pulling the free end.

Double Karabiner Brake

When a heavy load is being lowered and more friction is required a double karabiner brake can be used. This is operated and tied off exactly the same as a single brake.

ASSEMBLY OF KARABINER BRAKE
WITH CONTROL ROPE ABOVE

(i) HOLD KRAB IN RIGHT HAND
WITH THE GATE POINTING UP
AND ANTI CLOCKWISE. PUSH A
LOOP OF ROPE UP FROM BELOW
THROUGH THE KRAB. KEEP THE
LOAD ROPE NEAREST YOU.

(ii) HOLD THE SECOND KRAB
IN LEFT HAND IN THE SAME
POSITION AS THE FIRST AND
CLIP INTO THE BACK BAR OF
THE KRAB FROM ABOVE.

(iii) NOW CLIP THE SECOND
KRAB INTO OTHER SIDE OF
KRAB OVER THE GATE

KARABINER BRAKES

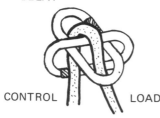

BELAY

CONTROL   LOAD

(i) CONTROL ROPE BELOW

CONTROL BELAY

LOAD

(ii) CONTROL ROPE ABOVE

TYING OFF A KRAB BRAKE

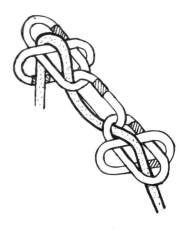

DOUBLE KARABINER BRAKE

Improvised Friction Brakes

There are several improvised friction brakes which can be used when karabiners are in short supply - the brake bar (Fig.i) from the crossed karabiner may be replaced by the shaft of a peg hammer (Fig.ii) or by a standard angle piton clipped into a karabiner and placed across (Fig.iv). Either of these methods are as efficient as the slide on brake bar which can be bought for this purpose.

When using an angle piton, it is important to check that there are no burrs or sharp edges which may catch on the rope. The piton must be longer than the longitudinal axis of the karabiner to prevent it sliding around and falling through the karabiner.
(Fig.iv P.152).

Karabiner Brake made with Non Screw Gate Karabiners

In certain circumstances screw gate karabiners may not be available and non screw gate karabiners may have to be used. The safest brake to use is made with four non screw gate karabiners. Superimpose two karabiners with back bars covering the gates to prevent the rope slipping out. Now assemble the brake in the normal way clipping one karabiner in from one side and one in from the other. This is a perfectly safe brake for abseiling and lowering if the normal operating instructions are followed. (Fig.iii page 152)

IMPROVISED FRICTION BRAKES

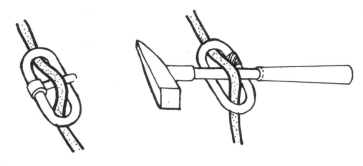

(i) KARABINER BRAKE BAR.   (ii) HAMMER SHAFT AND KRAB.

(iii) KARABINER BRAKE MADE WITH
NON SCREW GATE KRABS BACK
TO BACK.

(iv) ANGLE PITON USED
AS BRAKE BAR.

PASSING A KNOT THROUGH A KARABINER BRAKE

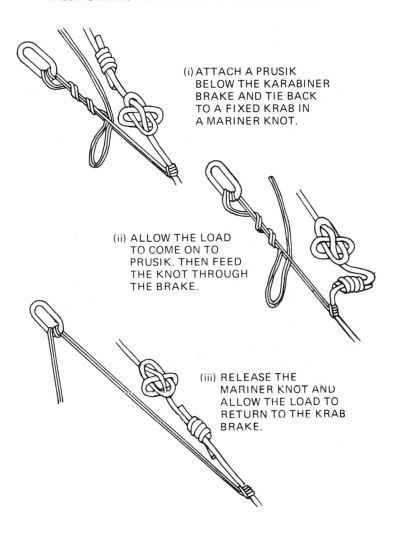

(i) ATTACH A PRUSIK BELOW THE KARABINER BRAKE AND TIE BACK TO A FIXED KRAB IN A MARINER KNOT.

(ii) ALLOW THE LOAD TO COME ON TO PRUSIK. THEN FEED THE KNOT THROUGH THE BRAKE.

(iii) RELEASE THE MARINER KNOT AND ALLOW THE LOAD TO RETURN TO THE KRAB BRAKE.

KARABINERS

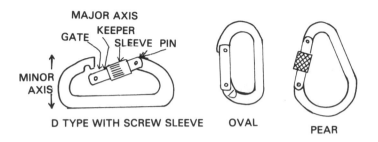

MAJOR AXIS
KEEPER
GATE **SLEEVE PIN**
MINOR AXIS

D TYPE WITH SCREW SLEEVE   OVAL   PEAR

REVERSED GATES

OPPOSING GATES

TO PROVIDE EXTRA SAFETY (c.f. SCREW SLEEVE) TWO KARABINERS
CAN BE USED WITH REVERSED OR OPPOSING GATES

154

THE ROBOT

The Robot is an interesting rappel/rescue device which has great versatility but has not been widely accepted by the climbing community. Its uses are as follows:

Rappel Mode

As a rappel device it can provide adjustable degrees of friction as can be seen in the diagrams on p.156. This allows it to use ropes of different diameters.

1. Rappel using double 9mm.
2. Rappel using double 11mm.
3. Rappel using 5 or 7mm. (emergency use)
4. Rappel using single 9mm. **page 157 (3).**

Rescue Mode

In the rescue mode, p. 157 (4), the device provides a one way system on the same principle as the Bachmann clutch and Garda knot.

ROBOT DEVICE — RAPPEL MODES

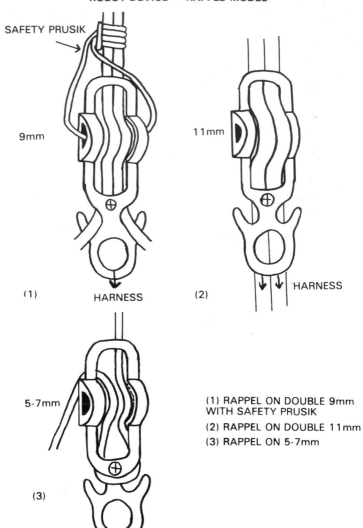

SAFETY PRUSIK

9mm

(1)   HARNESS

11mm

(2)   HARNESS

5-7mm

(3)

HARNESS

(1) RAPPEL ON DOUBLE 9mm
WITH SAFETY PRUSIK
(2) RAPPEL ON DOUBLE 11mm
(3) RAPPEL ON 5-7mm

ROBOT — RAPPEL/RESCUE DEVICE

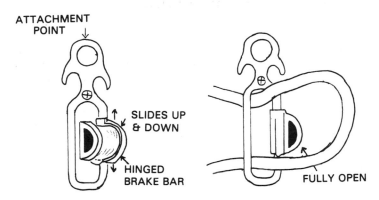

ATTACHMENT POINT

SLIDES UP & DOWN

HINGED BRAKE BAR

(1) ROBOT HALF OPEN

FULLY OPEN

(2) ROBOT OPEN AND LOOP OF ROPE FED THROUGH

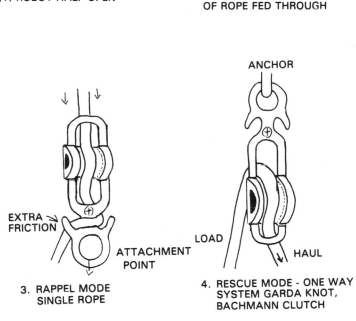

EXTRA FRICTION

ATTACHMENT POINT

3. RAPPEL MODE SINGLE ROPE

ANCHOR

LOAD

HAUL

4. RESCUE MODE - ONE WAY SYSTEM GARDA KNOT, BACHMANN CLUTCH

CHAPTER X
RAPPELLING

There are many different techniques of rappelling and the trend towards gadgets and descenders has affected rappelling as much as any other aspect of the sport of mountaineering. The three basic methods of rappelling are:

1. The classic method using the rope alone. A variation of this method is the arms rappel which is used on low angle slabs.
2. Methods improvised from standard climbing equipment - the karabiner brakes, angle pitons used as brake bars, friction hitches, see Chapter IX.
3. Purpose built devices such as the figure of 8 descender, Bankl plate, Sticht plate (modified with additional karabiner), the Robot, brake bars and multiple brake bars. Many of these devices are used for belaying and the reader is referred to the other relevant sections of the book.

Each method has pros and cons and the factors which should be considered are as follows:

1. Simplicity of use - can the rope be attached and removed without disconnecting the device from the harness, e.g. angle piton used as a brake bar.
2. Does it kink the rope?
3. Can it be jammed by catching clothing in the device?
4. Does it give sufficient friction and control?
5. Can it easily be tied off under load and be released under load?
6. Does it allow you to pass a knot, e.g. classic or arm rappel?
7. Does it overheat - is there sufficient metal to dissipate heat build up from friction?
8. Ease of use - speed of assembly - this is important in long alpine rappel descents where speed is important.
9. Does it automatically separate the ropes, e.g. the double Sticht plate/Bankl plate.
10. If it is unloaded can the system dissemble and jam up, e.g. the figure of 8 rappel can form a larks foot jamming the system.

ARM RAPPEL

CLASSIC RAPPEL

*SLABS ONLY

TO BRAKE SWING ARM X
ACROSS BODY AND INCREASE
ROPE/BODY CONTACT

Classic Rappel

PROS

1. Simple and quick for experts.
2. Requires no extra equipment.
3. Possible to rappel past knots in the rope.
4. Cannot jam up.

CONS

1. Beginners confuse correct rope positions.
2. Uncomfortable.
3. Dangerous to use on overhangs.
4. Centre of gravity at the crotch. Too low.
5. Awkward to set up when using a rucksack.

159

Overheating

The danger of overheating, point (7) is a consideration which may occur when:

1. The rappel is fast and the load heavy.
2. The rope is very dry. Relative humidity below 30% greatly increases heat generation.
3. The rope is coated with mud or impregnated with foreign particles.
4. The device already has friction grooves - they will heat quicker than devices with no friction grooves.
5. The devices are small with little mass to absorb heat. On the other hand a cool damp rope greatly reduces the likelihood of friction melting.

Classic Rappel

Generally speaking the carrying of specialized equipment by the ordinary climber is a waste of time and effort, especially if adequate methods of using standard equipment are available. All climbers should be able to rappel using the classic method which requires the rope only. This method is simple, there is no equipment to jam up or fail, and it is a simple method which allows one to rappel past a knot in the rope. Its main disadvantages are that it is uncomfortable requiring adequate padded clothing and leather palmed gloves, and it is extremely hazardous to use in a free rappel when one is not touching the rock since you turn upside down.

Body Position

The position of the body varies according to the angle of the rock and as a general rule is at an angle of 45° to the rock face. The feet are braced apart for stability and the knees are slightly flexed to act as shock absorbers. The body may be turned towards the lower controlling hand on the rope to facilitate observation of the descent route. The upper hand is to assist in maintaining the body position as a guide.

Negotiating of Overhangs and Roofs

Care must be exercised in descending past a roof. There are two alternatives:

i. A short bounding leap letting enough rope out to descend past the lip of the roof without smashing into it.

ii.   To turn sideways to the rock face with your hip on the lip of the overhang and your lower control hand away from the rock. From this position ease yourself down being careful not to trap the upper hand between the rope and the rock face.

Arm Rappel
This method is suitable for low angle slabs and involves a single rope wrap around both arms with the rope passing around the back of the body.

Multiple Rappels
The Italian guide Gervasutti and Scottish climber Tom Patey are but two of the more famous mountaineers who have been killed while rappelling: Gervasutti fell while attempting to retrieve a jammed abseil rope, Patey while attempting to unjam his descender in which the rope had pulled his shirt. Both men were experienced climbers and both were, as is the normal procedure, unbelayed while rappelling. This factor alone makes rappelling one of the most dangerous skills practiced by the mountaineer - he is vulnerable to anchor failure, rope failure, equipment failure, stone fall and lightning. In spite of these factors many people regard rappelling as fun and practice it as an activity in its own right. Rappelling is the basic skill used in descending rock, snow or ice which may be too difficult or dangerous or time consuming to climb down. By all means, perfect the technique, but if it can be avoided the alternative may be preferred. The purpose of this chapter is to outline a safe procedure when doing multiple rappel descents on a mountain.

The first requisite is to find a secure anchor - very often rappel points have fixed pins and loops of tape or rope in various states of decay. Always test the fixed pins with a hammer and if they are insecure remove and replace them. Never use the tape or slings unless they look very new as nylon deteriorates rapidly in ultraviolet light, which is stronger the higher you climb. If possible always use slings rather than placing the rope directly around a rock spike as it is more difficult to retrieve and increases the possibility of the rope jamming. When using rock spikes or rappel anchors blunt any sharp rock edges which may cut the belay sling using a piton hammer or a piece of rock. In the event of you running out of rappel slings it may be necessary in an emergency to cut off short lengths of the climbing rope for that purpose, although this expediency can only be used a few times. As a general rule it is better to have more than one anchor and these should be linked in such a way that they are equally loaded.

Each anchor point should be tied off separately to the suspension point of the rappel rope so that the failure of one anchor will not result in the shock loading of another.

Once the anchor points have been rigged the rappel ropes can be joined through the rappel sling(s). The joining knot should be the double fisherman's knot. Great care should be exercised in throwing the ropes down the cliff face to ensure that they will fall free and do not snag or jam on any rocks or cracks or tangle in themselves. There are several ways of doing this, depending on the terrain below. If the ground below is vertical pay out a loop of one rope from the rappel rope, keeping it neatly coiled in the hand. When you have about one third of the rope left in the hand or when the loop disappears from view throw the remaining coils horizontally out from the cliff face. When the ground is less steep pay out over half the rope onto the ledge in a pile, making sure that the rope pays out from the top and throw the remainder of the rope horizontally out from the cliff face. This normally pulls out the remaining rope clear of the face to give a clean rappel. Always coil the rope in small coils for ease of throwing and throw each rope separately, not together.

Some people prefer to butterfly the rope for throwing, i.e. loop it to and fro in a series of S's to be held in the hand or laid on the ledge. This takes more time but may in some instances be more efficient. As an extra precaution a knot may be tied in the end of each rappel rope to guard against rappelling off the end. In the U.S.A. some climbers tie a bong-bong, or large angle piton to the end of the rope to act as a stopper. These techniques do, however, increase the possibility of the rope snagging when it is thrown down the cliff face. On rare occasions, i.e. very strong winds blowing up or across the cliff face it may be impossible to throw the rope down. In these instances the climber will have to rappel holding both ropes in a coil and paying out a coil at a time - this technique does require a certain level of skill and should be practiced beforehand.

Once the rappel has been set up the first man to descend has a set procedure to follow. If the route is a well used descent route there is not too much of a problem, if it is a 'blind' descent certain precautions should be taken. The lead man could rappel on one rope tied off while being belayed on the second rope. In the event of no descent route being found he would carry prusik slings to enable him to climb back up the rope. The use of a safety rope while rappelling is time consuming and in mountaineering situations safety and speed are always in conflict. It is possible to safeguard a rappel by

(i) FIGURE OF 8 WHERE
    THE ROPE HAS SLIPPED
    FORWARD AND LOCKED
    IN A LARK'S FOOT

(ii) PREVENTION OF (i) BY CLIPP-
     ING ROPE
     INTO ATTACHMENT
     KARABINER X

(iii) FIGURE OF 8 TIED OFF
      WITH OVERHAND SLIP KNOT.
      PULL ON Y TO RELEASE
      UNDER LOAD.

(iv) FIGURE OF 8 WITH
     DOUBLE ROPE IN
     RAPPEL MODE.

attaching a prusik from a chest harness to the rappel rope and sliding
it down the rope with the upper hand. Always carry an extra prusik
in the event of the chest prusik jamming from premature loading -
the second prusik sling can be attached to the rope and stepped into
to facilitate the unloading and loosening of the chest prusik. This self
rescue method may also be used to rescue hair, clothing and rope
kinks which have been pulled into the rappel karabiner or descender
and jammed. One should, therefore always carry at least one prusik
sling when rappeling. Another method of safeguarding a rappel
when using a friction brake is to have a sling tied onto the rappel

163

SAFEGUARDING RAPPEL WITH PRUSIK BELOW THE KARABINER BRAKE

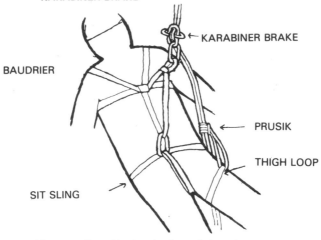

← KARABINER BRAKE

BAUDRIER

← PRUSIK

THIGH LOOP

SIT SLING

rope with a prusik or Penberthy knot **below** the friction brake. This safety sling is attached to the thigh and should be kept well below the brake to avoid jamming. When using this system it is desirable to rappel from a chest and seat harness combined with the friction brake at chest level well away from the safety prusik. On occasions it is useful to lock off the rappel. This is achieved by wrapping the lower free ropes around one leg two or three times.

The first man down on the rappel should clean any loose rock from the descent route, taking care not to dislodge them onto the rope below. When descending zones of loose rock, bounding leaps should be avoided as the vibrations on the rope above may dislodge rocks from the cliff face. Leaping and bounding on the rappel also imposes a greater strain on the anchor and causes rope abrasion and even cutting where the rope is in contact with sharp rock edges. The descent should be smooth and constant with the rappeller sideways onto the rock looking down to check his route of descent and occasionally looking up to check the rope above is not catching on rock projections. If a pendulum is involved great care must be exercised as the possiblity of the rope dislodging loose rock is greatly increased. When one has to execute a pendulum always start the pendulum above the point and gradually release more rope during the pendulum until you reach your destination. Once the correct

SAFEGUARDING A RAPPEL WITH A PRUSIK LOOP

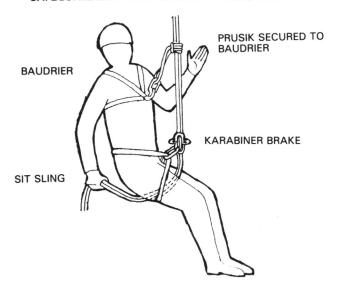

PRUSIK SECURED TO BAUDRIER

BAUDRIER

KARABINER BRAKE

SIT SLING

LOCKING OFF RAPPEL AND SEPARATING RAPPEL ROPES

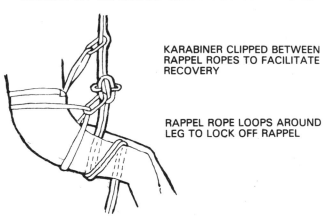

KARABINER CLIPPED BETWEEN RAPPEL ROPES TO FACILITATE RECOVERY

RAPPEL ROPE LOOPS AROUND LEG TO LOCK OFF RAPPEL

calculations have been made it may be advantageous to tie off the rappel rope so both hands are free to gain the ledge. Throughout the rappel a karabiner attached to the body harness or a gloved finger can be used to separate the two ropes on the descent thus facilitating their retrieval.

Once the first man has reached the rappel point he should check that 1) further descent is feasible, 2) the rappel rope is running free for ease of retrieval. The use of two ropes of different colours is useful here in order to distinguish which side the knot is on the rappel. Once these checks have been made the remainder of the party are ready to descend. If the descent is overhanging and involves a pendulum, the end of the rope should be secured to the new rappel point. When the party members have descended the rope should be pulled down steadily on the knotted side as a sudden jerk could cause the free end to flick around a projection or catch in a crack.

There are a few general observations to be made on rappelling to conclude this chapter. The ease of rappelling will depend on the type of stiffness of the rope - kernmantel normally runs more smoothly than hawser laid rope. The further down the rope the rappeller descends the less rope weight there is to assist in the friction braking and the more tightly he must hold the rope. When doing multiple rappels using friction devices be aware of overheating of metal parts used as the nylon rope may be damaged by melting. One should avoid rappelling at all cost in a lightning storm as a wet rope is an excellent conductor of electricity and the rappeller is in an extremely vulnerable position. As with all mountaineering skills, practice and experience are of paramount importance if one is to become proficient.

RECOVERING ICE SCREW ON A RAPPEL

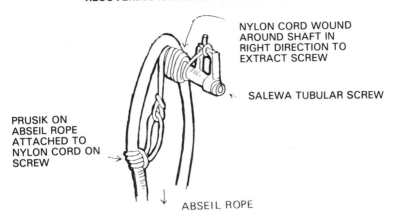

NYLON CORD WOUND AROUND SHAFT IN RIGHT DIRECTION TO EXTRACT SCREW

SALEWA TUBULAR SCREW

PRUSIK ON ABSEIL ROPE ATTACHED TO NYLON CORD ON SCREW

ABSEIL ROPE

RECOVERING AN ICE AXE ON A RAPPEL

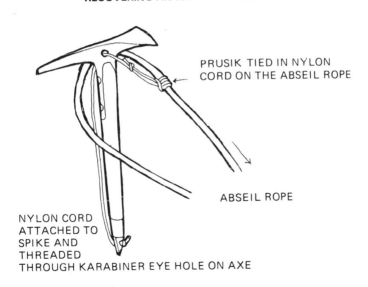

PRUSIK TIED IN NYLON CORD ON THE ABSEIL ROPE

ABSEIL ROPE

NYLON CORD ATTACHED TO SPIKE AND THREADED THROUGH KARABINER EYE HOLE ON AXE

167

Recovering an Ice Screw on a Rappel

An interesting method of recovering a Salewa tubular ice screw after it has been used for a rappel was demonstrated to me by the French guide Walter Cecchinal. The screw is inserted part way with the eye hole pointing upwards. A piece of ½" tape or nylon line is tied to the eye hole and wound round the shaft of the screw in the right direction to extract the screw. This is then attached to a prusik sling fastened to the rappel rope. When the rope is pulled the screw is rotated and extracted. It is important to have sufficient turns around the screw to ensure its complete extraction. This will vary according to the length of ice screw.

Recovering an Ice Axe on a Rappel

A similar method can be used to retrieve an ice axe after it has been used to reinforce a snow mushroom used as an abseil point. A nylon line is attached to the spike of the axe (some axes have a hole for this purpose) run up the shaft and threaded through the karabiner eye hole at the head of the axe. The line is attached one side of the rappel rope with a prusik sling. When the rope is pulled the axe is extracted by the sling. Care should be taken not to be hit by the falling axe during the retrieval operation.

CHAPTER XI

IMPROVISED STRETCHERS AND CARRIES

An accident occurs in remote wilderness, far from normal life support systems. You administer the necessary first aid. But now you are faced with the decision of whether to send a messenger for help and stay put, or to attempt to evacuate the casualty yourself.

The decision to stay put depends on the effect on the victim, and the nature of his injuries, and whether the party possesses sufficient resources to provide the injured individual with warm, dry shelter. Or a rapid rescue response comes from sending the messenger for help, or from, say, search and rescue authorities responding automatically to an incomplete trip plan, if one has been left at home base.

The decision to move a casualty is a serious one, and depends primarily on the victim's injuries because there is a distinct possibility that injuries may be aggravated and worsened by rough, unskilled evacuation technique.

As a general rule, avoid moving the casualty until you have undertaken a thorough examination of his injuries because movement of a person with a spinal injury may result in paralysis.

If the person is only slightly injured, and is strong and in reasonable spirits, he might well be able to assist in his own evacuation. This self-aided approach should be used whenever possible because it greatly relieves the load on the rescuer(s), and is often beneficial psychologically to the casualty. The casualty can be relieved of his pack, and his load can be divided among others in the party. One person can walk alongside the injured person, giving both physical (shoulder crutch) and psychological support. If necessary, a second person can break trail ahead. A stout walking staff or improvised single crutch may be used to assist the casualty. If a crutch is used, it should be about 16 inches shorter than the person's height, and should have a good handgrip to ease the load on the victim's armpit. If a crutch is too long, it will be uncomfortable, and there is possibility of damage to the radial nerve in the armpit. When using a crutch, the casualty supports his weight on the palm of his hand, not his armpit.

Differentiation

It is important to differentiate between (1) emergency movement
169

from life-threatening situations involving short distances up to 50 yards, (2) short-term carries of up to several hundred yards, normally from an exposed location to a more sheltered spot, and (3) emergency evacuation to medical assistance over a number of miles.

In many instances, emergency movement and short-term carries are similar techniques, although as the length of the carry increases, improvised equipment is required to take the weight off the carriers' arms. The effectiveness of these carries depends on the terrain, the fitness of the carrier(s) and the weight, physical conditon, and the severity of injuries of the casualty.

Solo Carries

There are several emergency movement techniques a solitary rescuer can use on an unconscious casualty in a life-threatening situation.

The simple drag is accomplished by grabbing hold of the casualty by the collar, cradling his head between the forearms, and pulling him headfirst away from the hazard, i.e. fire, position exposed to gunfire, etc. This is the quickest and easiest method, and has the advantage of putting traction on the spine. Care should be taken to avoid twisting or turning the victim's body, or bumping it over irregular terrain.

There are three simple one-man carries that can be used with unconscious or conscious casualties. One is the cradle carry in which the casualty is held under the armpits and under the legs across the carrier's chest. This is possible only with lightweight casualties.

The packstrap carry, in which the rescuer carries the casualty in the prone position on his back, with his arms over his shoulders, is the second method.

Third is the fireman's lift, in which the victim is carried face down over one shoulder, and is held by the carrier's arm through the casualty's legs, gripping onto the casualty's arm. This allows the carrier one free arm for security, i.e., grasping the rungs of a ladder, safety line, or a weapon.

When lifting casualties, it is helpful if they can be propped against a rock or tree, and the carrier can squat, using his leg muscles to lift the victim while keeping his back as straight as possible. Lifting an unconscious person requires skill, and should be practiced carefully in safe situations in order to avoid injury to oneself.

The one-man improvised carry may be adequate when the casualty is light, slightly injured, and the distance is short and over easy

170

IMPROVISED CARRIES

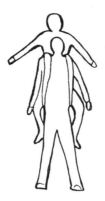

ONE MAN SPLIT ROPE CARRY

CROSSED SLINGS
AND POLE CARRY

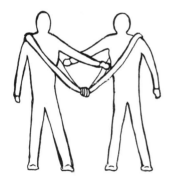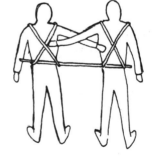

TWO MAN SPLIT ROPE CARRY   TWO MAN SLING AND POLE CARRY

terrain. The pickaback (piggyback) carry is the simplest method, but is physically demanding, and there are a variety of improvised techniques to take the strain off the carrier's arms. The backpack carry is a practical modification of the pickaback, with the carrier wearing an empty backpack, and the casualty's legs going through the extended shoulder straps at the carrier's hips. A well-padded pole can be passed horizontally through the lower part of the backpack straps, providing support for the casualty's legs. A rope can be split into two loops, then the casualty's legs placed in the loops which are carried over the rescuer's shoulders. Rope slings or tape can be used to support the cross pole in the absence of a backpack.

Two-Man Carries

When a greater number of rescuers are available, the two-man carries, using the previously cited techniques, may be less tiring. In the two-man carry, a 6 to 7 foot pole is padded and inserted behind the base of the straps of two backpacks, leaving a 2-foot gap in the middle on which the casualty can sit. If no rucksacks are available, split ropes or slings of rope or tape may be improvised to support the pole. This carry does require carriers to be of similar height, and also demands a broad trail because three people must travel abreast. This carry is also difficult to use while traversing slopes. Two-man carriers using single seats made by clasping hands can be used for a short distance.

Improvised Stretchers
Pigott Rope Stretcher -

The most common improvised stretcher know today is the Pigott Rope stretcher. It consists of a length of No.2 rope usually tied off in a series of loops with the overhand knot. The spare rope runs down joining the ends of the loops to form the side of the stretcher. Instead of using the old method of joining the loops by doubling the ends and laboriously threading the rope through, a sheet bend may be tied. In order to facilitate tying the knot, hold the rope in coils. The cross loops can be reinforced by running the spare rope down the centre of the stretcher and tying to each one with an overhand knot. The stretcher should then be turned over so that the knots do not dig into the casualty's back. In any event the rope stretcher should be well padded for the casualty's comfort. It is possible for an experienced person to construct a Pigott using this method in less than fifteen minutes.

IMPROVISED PIGOTT STRETCHER

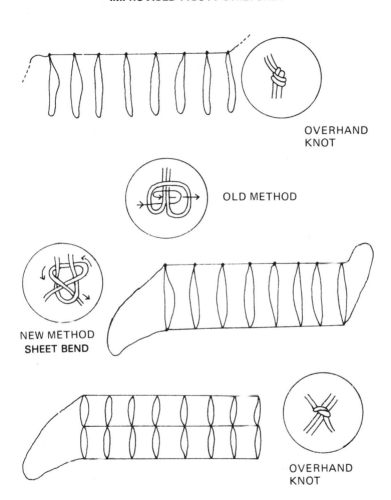

OVERHAND
KNOT

OLD METHOD

NEW METHOD
SHEET BEND

OVERHAND
KNOT

ALPINE BASKET

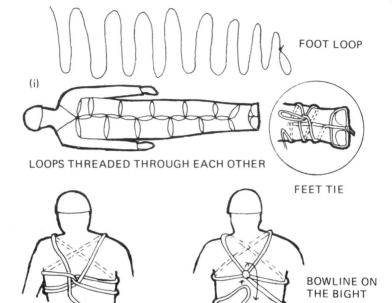

FOOT LOOP

(i)

LOOPS THREADED THROUGH EACH OTHER

FEET TIE

(i)

TIE OFF FOR THE CHEST

(ii)

BOWLINE ON THE BIGHT

SECOND METHOD STARTING FROM THE CHEST AND LACING TO THE FEET

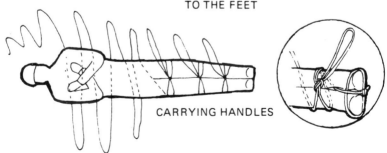

CARRYING HANDLES

(iii) THIRD METHOD TIE OFF LONGER LOOPS WITH A SHEET BEND

174

The Alpine Basket -

The Alpine rope basket is an even quicker way of constructing an emergency stretcher although initally designed as a lowering cradle in improvised cliff rescues. There are three methods of construction.

i.   A loop for the feet is tied in the end of the rope which is then laid down in a series of S shaped loops on the ground. The patient is placed on the loops which are laced through one another from the feet to the chest leaving the arms outside. The top is tied off as a chest harness crossed at the back and the spare rope is used to provide carrying handles.

ii. The next method is to tie a bowline on the bight to give two loops which are used as a chest harness, the casualty is then laced on in the normal manner and tied off at the feet. It is important that the first loops be threaded through the top of the chest tie. This method is quicker and easier than the Pigott.

iii. The third method is - lay down a series of loops much longer than in methods one and two and to offset the casualty on the loops. The longer loop is then tied off on the opposite short loop in a sheet bend and the long bight can then be used as a carrying handle.

Both the Pigott and the rope basket lack rigidity and are consequently difficult to carry and they cannot be used for spinal injuries. They may be improved by adding rigidity in the form of crossed ice axes lashed together and well padded. Pack frames may be used to reinforce the stretcher or can be leashed and splinted together to form a rigid carrying platform. If there are some long poles available, e.g. tent poles, skis, a rope laced stretcher can be constructed. The knots on the stretcher poles may be overhand on the bight or clove hitches. Transverse rigidity may be obtained by lashing cross members at the head and foot of the stretcher. It is possible to use two anoraks with poles through the sleeves to make a stretcher when no rope is available.

There are of course many improvisations possible, depending on the materials available at the time, and there is little doubt that quite long carries can be undertaken with well built, rigid, improvised stretchers. Rope stretchers and individual carrying methods can only be used for short carries. Always remember the limitations as well as the advantages of the improvised carrying techniques when you are considering using them.

IMPROVISED STRETCHERS

OVERHAND KNOT

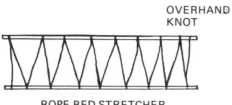

ROPE BED STRETCHER

CLOVE HITCH

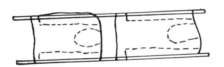

POLES

STRETCHER MADE FROM TWO ANORAKS

POLE

CASUALTY'S WEIGHT HOLDS FOLDED GROUND SHEET IN POSITION

STRETCHER MADE FROM GROUND SHEET

Construction: Rope Stretcher

1. Lay out the rope from the centre in a series of parallel S's.
2. The width of the S's must be no wider than the width of the casualty, this is important to produce maximum rigidity. The length of the S's should be as long as the casualty, approximately 16 S bends.
3. Bring the rope ends around the side of the stretcher and tie a clove at each apex of the bend in the S. Leave a small loop to thread ropes and/or poles through. There should be approx. 4″-6″ between each loop.
4. The remaining rope is run through the loops at the site of the clove hitch. Secure.

Optional: At this point it is recommended that a rigid pole (i.e. ski poles, skis, ice axes, tress) be run through the loops. This will provide greater rigidity and stability making the stretcher more comfortable and easier to carry.

5. At least six people are needed to carry the stretcher effectively:
   Two at the head.
   Two at the feet.
   Two in the middle.
6. Pad the stretcher well with available materials. Use a spare rope to secure the casualty.

Pros:
- Two man construction taking approximately 15 minutes.
- Uses materials that one would normally carry on a trip.
- Reasonably comfortable.
- Can be reinforced with ski poles, trees, etc.

Cons:
- Provides relatively little rigidity.
- *Must* not be used for spinal injuries.
- Group must be aware of methods of construction to save time and provide maximum rigidity.
- Many people (6-8) are needed to carry the stretcher.
- The rope stretcher is difficult to carry over long distances.

ROPE STRETCHER

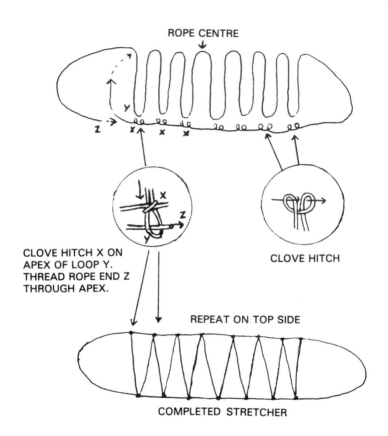

ROPE CENTRE

CLOVE HITCH X ON
APEX OF LOOP Y.
THREAD ROPE END Z
THROUGH APEX.

CLOVE HITCH

REPEAT ON TOP SIDE

COMPLETED STRETCHER

The Travois
The travois is basically a branch stretcher with the branches left on at one end of the stretcher poles and used as a cushioned drag. For the travois two small trees are cut and laid parallel about eighteen inches apart. The branches are stripped from the upper side, those underneath are left to cushion the ride and to aid braking. Two crossbraces are lashed across the trunks about 6ft apart. A rope is used for diagonal bracing then laced zig-zag from side to side to form a bed. The casualty is placed in this improvised bed and strapped in if necessary or warranted. The butt ends can be placed in the rescuers pack straps whilst moving forward.

Advantages:
- Ability to carry heavy loads with minimal energy expenditure and limited manpower.
- One rescuer under ideal conditions can facilitate transportation of a casualty.
- Simply constructed - easy to make.
- No need to carry extra gear.

Disadvantages:
- Rarity of usable trees at high altitudes.
- Limited to areas of specialized resources.
- Varied topographical limitations.
- Difficulty facilitating traverse on steeper slopes.

Ski Travois: A variation of the travois is the ski travois contructed by lashing four skis together with two cross struts as shown in the diagram.

Plastic Sled - Improvised Ski Stretcher
This technique provides an effective means of transporting victims in winter conditions, while utilizing a nominal amount of inexpensive equipment.

Equipment:
- children's plastic sled (pliable) or plastic carpet
- ensolite pad
- nylon ropes/polypropylene cord
- skis
- sleeping bag

SKI STRETCHERS AND TRAVOIS

PLASTIC SLED

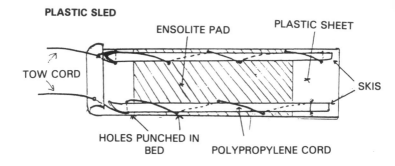

ENSOLITE PAD

PLASTIC SHEET

TOW CORD

SKIS

HOLES PUNCHED IN BED

POLYPROPYLENE CORD

SKI TRAVOIS

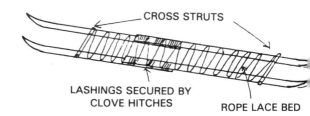

CROSS STRUTS

LASHINGS SECURED BY CLOVE HITCHES

ROPE LACE BED

TRAVOIS

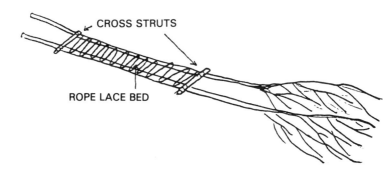

CROSS STRUTS

ROPE LACE BED

Construction:-
- cut holes in ensolite pad and plastic sled in identical areas
- place ensolite on plastic sled and align holes
- feed rope through holes, alternating from top to bottom
- place skis underneath the ensolite in direction of pull
- ski poles may also be used to provide extra support or serve as splints
- sleeping bag is placed over ensolite pad and may be covered with a waterproof layer

Pros:	Cons
inexpensive	support is not adequate for
simple to construct	spinal injuries
lightweight	requires snow
comfortable	cannot be used on steep grades
provides some support	
easy to transport victim	

Organization of Stretcher Carry

a. Division of Labour

Leader (i) Appoint a leader to organize and take charge of the evacuation.

Carriers (ii) Appoint carriers. Three pairs matched in height and weight across the stretcher. The tallest at the feet and the shortest at the head to ensure a slight head down position of the casualty. Each carrier should be numbered to facilitate change over on the move. Each carrier should have a webbing sling improvisation which transfers the weight of the stretcher to his shoulders and back.

Others (iii) If there is sufficient man power a second team of carriers should be appointed and given numbers corresponding to the first team. They should know their position on the stretcher. Other spare people should act as scouts selecting the easiest route ahead and clearing obstacles where possible. The remainder of the party should act as supply carriers transporting the stretcher carriers equipment.

b. Rotation of Roles

(i) The leader is responsible for calling rest periods every 10-20 minutes or when required.

(ii) The leader is responsible for organizing a rotation of duties to minimize fatigue and distribute the work load evenly.

(iii) A well organized team can change over bearers *whilst on the move* by exchanging one bearer at a time on the leaders command.

c.   The Stretcher

(i)   The casualty *MUST* be checked at frequent intervals by a designated person.

(ii)   The casualty should be securely fastened into the stretcher.

(iii)   Difficult obstacles - ditches, boulders, fences, dead fall may best be tackled by passing the stretcher hand over hand from one set of bearers to another stationed on the other side of the obstacle.

(iv)   Great care should be taken to ensure the comfort of the casualty. If his condition is deteriorating due to the carry it may be necessary to stop and stabilize his condition before proceeding. Remember, each situation must be considered as uniquely different and you may face a 'no win' situation e.g. to evacuate will aggravate the casualty's condition; to remain and await help will increase the time before expert medical service is available when it may be urgently required. In the final analysis one can only do one's best according to the circumstances.

BRANCH STRETCHER

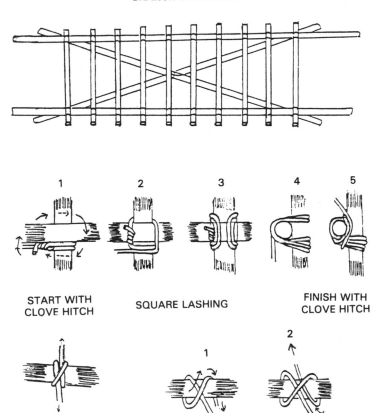

1 2 3 4 5

START WITH
CLOVE HITCH

SQUARE LASHING

FINISH WITH
CLOVE HITCH

FINISHED   KNOT

1

2

CHAPTER XII

CREVASSE RESCUE

The greatest danger of glacier travel to the mountaineer is a fall into a crevasse. The correct procedure to follow in dealing with this hazard is:

1. KNOWLEDGE/AWARENESS. Acquire a detailed knowledge of glacial topography and crevasse formation and location.
2. AVOIDANCE. Careful route planning using maps, aerial photographs, local experts and prior reconnaissance from safe vantage points using field glasses.
3. PRECAUTIONS/PREPARATION
    a. Always rope up on glacier
    b. Travel in a party of 3 or more or 2 parties of 2
    c. Wear a full harness, carry prusiks, pulley, karabiners, and an ice screw and snow anchor.
4. MANAGEMENT. Be thoroughly knowledgeable and trained in basic crevasse rescue techniques.

This article is really concerned with stages (3) and (4).

Preparation for Glacial Travel
Tying In.   All climbers should wear a full body harness or chest and seat harness when crossing a glacier. The chest and seat harness should be fastened together with a short length of tensile rope 7-9mm diameter wrapped several times for strength. The climbing rope should preferably be 11mm diameter, tied with a figure of 8 on the bight and clipped into the front tie of the harness with a screw gate karabiner. This is contrary to standard tie in practice where the karabiner is omitted as an extra and possibly weak link in the chain. Falls into crevasses are generally less severe than climbing falls due to the rope cutting into the lip. This fact and the need for the rescuer to be able to detach himself easily from the system support the use of a screw gate karabiner (UIAA approved) attachment. Finally two prusik loops 6-7mm diameter and 5 meters long are attached to the rope by prusik knots and tucked away behind the chest harness.

Glacial Travel
When travelling over crevassed terrain *keep THE ROPE TAUT* at all times and *DO NOT* travel with coils in the hand. In most instances falls can be arrested before the climber/skier goes completely in to the crevasse if the rope is taut and his companions are alert. In extremely

dangerous crevassed terrain it may be safer to anchor and belay each person although this is very time consuming.

ROPE LENGTHS   THE RULE OF THIRDS
(1) TWO MAN PARTY - 50 METRE ROPE 11mm DIAMETER

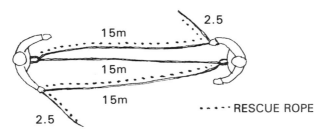

2.5

15m

15m

15m

2.5

----- RESCUE ROPE

(A) Run ropes through karabiners on chest harness and move apart to set correct distance.

(B) The 2.5. metres either end allow for rope stretch in the rescue.

(C) When the correct distances are reached each man ties off the rope on his harness karabiner leaving him 15 metres from his companion. The spare 15 metres are coiled and carried in the rucksack ready for rescue.

(2) THREE MAN PARTY - this is the recommended minimum number for safe glacier travel - 50 METRE ROPE 11mm DIAMETER.

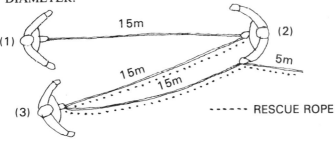

(1) 15m (2)

5m

15m

15m

(3) ----- RESCUE ROPE

In this instance 5 metres is added to the spare rope from the number man to allow for rope stretch in the rescue.

(3) FOUR MAN PARTY

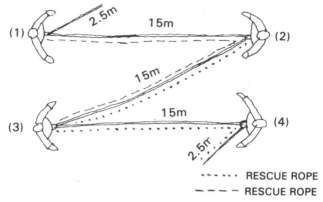

······ RESCUE ROPE

– – – – RESCUE ROPE

In this instance 2.5 metres is added to either end to allow for rope stretch in the rescue.

The attachment of more than four persons to a rope for glacier travel is undesirable due to the shortening of the rope interval between climbers and the increasing difficulty of co-ordinating the rate of travel of the group.

TWO MAN PARTY - 40 METRES OF 9mm DIAMETER ROPE DOUBLED

A recent innovation has been the use of 40 metres of 9mm diameter rope used as a double rope for glacier travel. The rope is doubled and one climber ties in the middle of the rope and the other ties into the two free ends. In the event of a fall into a crevasse one rope can be used to hold the victim whilst the other is available for rescue.

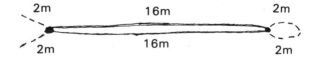

CREVASSE RESCUE SYSTEM WITH ONE SECURE ANCHOR

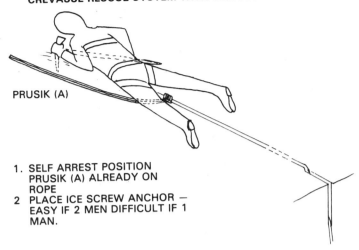

PRUSIK (A)

1. SELF ARREST POSITION PRUSIK (A) ALREADY ON ROPE
2. PLACE ICE SCREW ANCHOR — EASY IF 2 MEN DIFFICULT IF 1 MAN.

Crevasse rescue management

(1) When partner falls into crevasse immediately drop to ground in self arrest position on a tight rope. Self arrest position is axe across the chest, pick facing down, feet apart with toes jammed into snow surface. This should be practiced under simulated load conditions.

Place a secure anchor, an ice axe or ice screw depending on the depth of snow on the glacier. This is difficult for one person to do on his/her own when in the self arrest position and is the *primary reason why a party of three is recommended* since the third man could do this relatively easily.

Under different snow conditions a deadman anchor, skis, or a buried pack may by used as alternative anchor points. The snow may be packed around the buried anchor if it is very soft and/or additional people may stand on the anchor for security. The provision of a secure anchor is absolutely essential for a safe rescue.

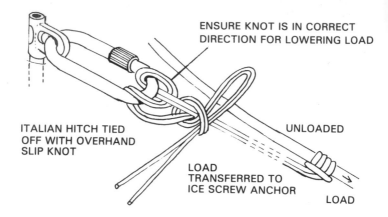

ENSURE KNOT IS IN CORRECT
DIRECTION FOR LOWERING LOAD

ITALIAN HITCH TIED
OFF WITH OVERHAND
SLIP KNOT

UNLOADED

LOAD
TRANSFERRED TO
ICE SCREW ANCHOR

LOAD

(2) Once the anchor is placed tie in the prusik line on the anchor karabiner with an Italian hitch and tie this knot off with an overhang slip knot.

If the Italian hitch is not in the correct direction for lowering the load it may be difficult to reverse and release under load. This method allows the system to be released even though the load is applied. - *Ability to release systems under load* is a recurring requirement of rescue systems.

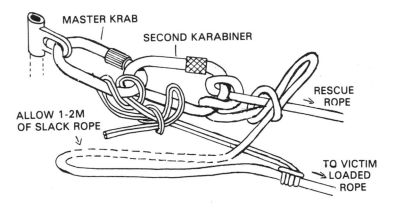

MASTER KRAB
SECOND KARABINER
RESCUE ROPE
ALLOW 1-2M OF SLACK ROPE
TO VICTIM LOADED ROPE

(3) Clip in a second karabiner to the master krab. Fasten main rope with Italian hitch and overhang slip knot.

This allows the release of the system under load as in stage (2). It is also a much stronger anchor than the prusik alone and allows the load rope to be used as a 'back-up belay' to the crevasse rescue system if the man power is available to operate it.

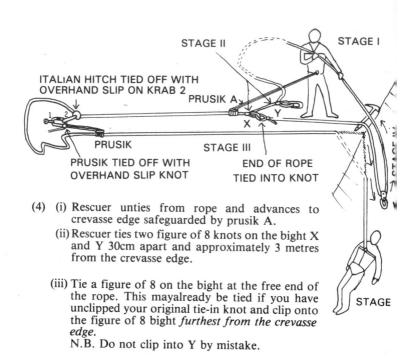

ITALIAN HITCH TIED OFF WITH
OVERHAND SLIP ON KRAB 2

STAGE II

STAGE I

PRUSIK A

PRUSIK

X Y

STAGE III

PRUSIK TIED OFF WITH
OVERHAND SLIP KNOT

END OF ROPE
TIED INTO KNOT

STAGE

(4) (i) Rescuer unties from rope and advances to crevasse edge safeguarded by prusik A.

   (ii) Rescuer ties two figure of 8 knots on the bight X and Y 30cm apart and approximately 3 metres from the crevasse edge.

   (iii) Tie a figure of 8 on the bight at the free end of the rope. This may already be tied if you have unclipped your original tie-in knot and clip onto the figure of 8 bight *furthest from the crevasse edge.*
   N.B. Do not clip into Y by mistake.

   (iv) Clip a pulley and krab onto the long rope loop formed by (iii) and lower to the victim. If necessary cut away the crevasse lip to remove soft snow.

   (v) The victim clips the pulley/krab into his harness and the rescuer pulls up the slack rope putting tension on the main anchor figure of 8 on the bight X. The main anchor/figure of 8 bight X and victim must be in *a straight direct line of pull.* If there are sufficient rescuers, the victim can be pulled out using this method. The victim can also assist by pulling up on one side of the pulley rope.

STAGE(i)   When no additional man power is available the hoist rope is taken back to figure of 8 Y and attached to a one way Garda knot.

N.B.   Check it is running in right direction and locking feedback of pulley rope before loading system.

STAGE (ii)   Attach a prusik V to the hoist rope and clip rope through with a krab to provide a 3-1 advantage.

N.B.   Do not confuse ropes and attach prusik V to rescue rope tied into figure of 8 bight Y.

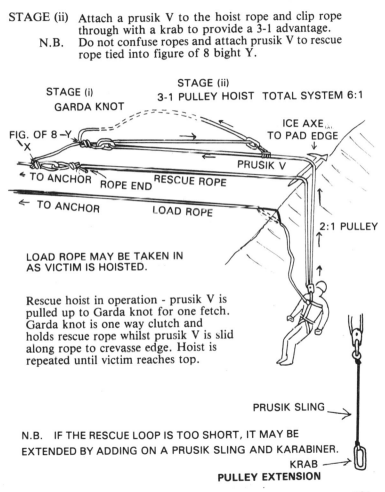

STAGE (i)
GARDA KNOT

STAGE (ii)
3-1 PULLEY HOIST TOTAL SYSTEM 6:1

ICE AXE
TO PAD EDGE

FIG. OF 8 –Y
X

PRUSIK V

TO ANCHOR   ROPE END   RESCUE ROPE

TO ANCHOR   LOAD ROPE

2:1 PULLEY

LOAD ROPE MAY BE TAKEN IN
AS VICTIM IS HOISTED.

Rescue hoist in operation - prusik V is
pulled up to Garda knot for one fetch.
Garda knot is one way clutch and
holds rescue rope whilst prusik V is slid
along rope to crevasse edge. Hoist is
repeated until victim reaches top.

PRUSIK SLING

N.B.   IF THE RESCUE LOOP IS TOO SHORT, IT MAY BE
EXTENDED BY ADDING ON A PRUSIK SLING AND KARABINER.

KRAB
PULLEY EXTENSION

FURTHER CONSIDERATIONS

(after Tim Auger, Public Safety Warden, Banff National Park)

There is little doubt that crevasse rescue is a strenuous and technically difficult undertaking and every situation should be reviewed to ascertain if the victim can climb out or be lowered to a ledge or floor from where he can traverse, stem or otherwise climb out. Modern ice climbing equipment can make this a feasible possibility. The 'dropped loop' system of crevasse rescue described has the apparent disadvantage that it seems complicated, however, this must be weighed against the following advantages.

1. Variations of the same system can be utilized in all circumstances regardless of the number of climbers present.

2. The rope used to rescue the victim, 'the dropped loop' is completely separate from the loaded rope holding the victim so the edge can be carefully prepared by padding with a rucksack or cutting away the soft snow. In the latter case avoid showering debris on the victim. The original rope which has cut into the crevasse lip may be able to be moved and a pad placed there once the tension has been relieved by the first hoist.

3. In the dropped loop system the victim can significantly assist the hoist by pulling up on the 'standing' rope he is hanging on while the rescuers pull on the other leg of the rope.

4. In this system the dropped loop portion of the rope can be used to recover packs and equipment before pulling up the victim.

5. In parties with more members the dropped loop system can be used to simply yard the victim out without the addition of the 3:1 pulley hoist.

6. If someone is available he can belay the victim on the original line to:
   a. safeguard him from falls,
   b. take his weight if required while adjusting the dropped loop.

7. The drop loop system has 'built in controls'. In the event of the victim being inadvertently pulled up against the crevasse wall by the rope sawing into the crevasse edge while hoisting, the system may be released. The one way hoist system of the Garda knot can be over-ridden by releasing the overhand slip knot locking the Italian hitch on the master karabiner on the original rope.

The whole system can then be lowered from this point and locked off again as required.

. disadvantage of the dropped loop system is that the victim must be c nscious to be able to connect into the pulley and karabiner. In the e ent of the victim being unable to do this then it will be necessa v for the rescuer to rappel down and clip him in, prusik out, and then effect the rescue! In conclusion crevasse rescue is an essential skill for the mountaineer and it is important that he/she acquaint themselves with the necessary skills to deal with the variety of situations they may be faced with in glacier travel.

THE ESSENTIAL RESCUE TECHNIQUES

The information explosion and the increasing pace of technology threatens to overwhelm the expert and neophyte alike in today's modern mountaineering. It is appropriate to conclude this book with a summation of the basic rescue techniques.

Essential Knowledge

1. A knot which grips under load and can be released and moved along the rope when unloaded - PRUSIK, KLEMHEIST, etc.
2. A knot which can be tied under load - ROUND TURN AND TWO HALF HITCHES (IF TIED OFF WITH OVERHAND SLIP KNOT CAN BE RELEASED UNDER LOAD).
3. A knot which can be released under load - ITALIAN HITCH TIED OFF WITH OVERHAND SLIP KNOT, MARINER KNOT.
4. A knot which gives a one-way clutch system - BACHMANN/PULLEY, GARDA KNOT, STUFFEL HITCH
5. Mechanics of pulley systems.
6. Knowledge of centre of gravity/point of suspension.
7. Self equalising anchor systems.
8. On Belay/Lowering/Rappel system.

Principles of Rescue

1. Always have a second back up.
2. Always have secure anchors.
3. Always double check everything.
4. Always plan ahead - know how to correct your mistakes.
5. Practice problems/solutions in controlled situations.
6. Carry a sharp pocket knife at all times.

Conclusion

Mountaineering is without doubt one of the most powerful of human activities in that it bestows an awesome freedom on the individual concerning his own destiny. This freedom should be matched with an even stronger sense of responsibility to self, to other climbers, and to society. It is intrinsic in the nature of the activity that climbers should be independent and capable of handling as far as possible their own problems and emergencies. This book hopefully provides the technical knowledge to help the individual climber achieve that aim.

NOTES

CICERONE CLIMBING & SCRAMBLING GUIDES

SCRAMBLES IN THE LAKE DISTRICT
R.B. Evans
ISBN 0 902363 39 5 192pp PVC cover £9.99
MORE SCRAMBLES IN THE LAKE DISTRICT   *R.B.Evans*
ISBN 1 85284 042 0 200 pp PVC cover £9.99
Exciting rock scrambles in gills or easy angled craglets, to thrill the mountaineer.

WINTER CLIMBS IN THE LAKE DISTRICT   Bob Bennett, Bill Birkett, and Brian Davison Brian Davison A new edition packed with the latest routes which confirm the area as a major winter climbing venue.   *ISBN 1 85284 246 6 200pp £14.99*

CLWYD ROCK Gary Dickinson. Rock climbs on the Welsh Border, around Wrexham and Llangollen. *ISBN 1 85284 094 3 232pp PVC cover £14.99*

SCRAMBLES IN SNOWDONIA   Steve Ashton The classic rock ridges and other adventurous routes up challenging rocky faces. Second edition. *ISBN 1 85284 088 9 168pp PVC cover £9.99*

WELSH WINTER CLIMBS Malcolm Campbell &Andy Newton The snow and ice climbs of North Wales. Superb diagrams and colour photos. *ISBN 1 85284 001 3 256pp PVC cover £14.99*

WEST MIDLANDS ROCK Doug Kerr The latest guide to the popular crags. *ISBN 1 85284 200 8 168pp £7.99*

CORNISH ROCK Rowland Edwards & Tim Dennell A superb photo topo guide to West Penwith, the most popular climbing in Cornwall, by the area's leading activists. *ISBN 1 85284 208 3 272pp A5 size Casebound £18.99*

CAIRNGORMS Winter Climbs   Allen Fyffe Covers the classic winter climbs in the Cairngorms, Lochnagar and Creag Meaghaidh.   *ISBN 0 902363 99 9   120pp PVC cover   £7.99*

THE ISLAND OF RHUM - A Guide for Walkers, Climbers and Visitors Hamish M.Brown The complete companion for any visitor to the island, owned by the Nature Conservancy.
ISBN 1 85284 002 1   100pp   £5.99

SCRAMBLES IN LOCHABER Noel Williams Some of the best scrambling in Britain around Glencoe and Ben Nevis and much of the Western Highlands around Fort William. *ISBN 1 85284 234 2 Revised edition 192pp £9.99*

SCRAMBLES IN SKYE J.W.Parker The Cuillins is a paradise for scrambling. The unique large scale 4-colour map which accompanies the book is the clearest available for this complex area. *ISBN 0 902363 38 7 144pp PVC cover   £9.99*

WINTER CLIMBS BEN NEVIS & GLENCOE Alan Kimber   Britain's finest winter climbing area. *ISBN 1 85284 179 6 232pp PVC cover £14.99*

FRENCH ROCK Bill Birkett THE guide to many exciting French crags! Masses of photo topos, with selected hit-routes in detail. *ISBN 1 85284 113 3. 332pp A5 size. £14.99*

Selected ROCK CLIMBS IN BELGIUM & LUXEMBOURG Chris Craggs Perfect rock, good protection and not too hot to climb in summer. *ISBN 1 85284 155 9 188p   A5 £12.99*

ROCK CLIMBS IN THE VERDON. An Introduction Rick Newcombe An English-style guide, which makes for easier identification of the routes and descents. *ISBN 1 85284 015 3 72pp £5.50*

ROCK CLIMBS IN THE PYRENEES Derek Walker The first English guide to these impressive climbs. Includes Pic du Midi d'Ossau and the Vignemale in France, and the Ordesa Canyon and Riglos in Spain. *ISBN 1 85284 039 0 168pp PVC cover £9.99*

ANDALUSIAN ROCK CLIMBS   Chris Craggs El Chorro and El Torcal are world famous. Includes Tenerife. *ISBN 1 85284 109 5 168pp £6.99*

COSTA BLANCA ROCK Chris Craggs Over 1500 routes on over 40 crags, many for the first time in English. The most comprehensive guide to the area. *ISBN 1 85284 241 5 240pp £12.99*

ROCK CLIMBS IN MAJORCA, IBIZA & TENERIFE *Chris Craggs* Holiday island cragging at its best. *ISBN 1 85284 189 3 240pp £10.99*

WALKS & CLIMBS IN THE PICOS DE EUROPA *Robin Walker* A definitive guide to these unique mountains. Walks and rock climbs of all grades. *ISBN 1 85284 033 1 232pp PVC cover £10.99*

KLETTERSTEIG Scrambles in the Northern Limestone Alps *Paul Werner Translated by Dieter Pevsner* Protected climbing paths similar to the Via Ferrata of the Dolomites. *ISBN 0 902363 46 8 184pp PVC cover £7.99*

THE CENTRAL APENNINES OF ITALY Walks, Scrambles and Climbs *Stephen Fox* The mountainous spine of Italy, with secluded walks, rock climbs and scrambles on the Gran Sasso d'Italia, and some of Italy's finest sport climbing crags. *ISBN 1 85284 219 9*

ITALIAN ROCK. Selected Climbs in Northern Italy *Al Churcher.* Val d'Orco and Mello, Lecco and Finale etc. *ISBN 0 902363 93 X 200pp PVC cover £8.99*

VIA FERRATA SCRAMBLES IN THE DOLOMITES *Höfler/Werner Translated by Cecil Davies.* The most exciting walks in the world. Wires, stemples and ladders enable the 'walker' to enter the climber's vertical environment. *ISBN 1 85284 089 7 248pp PVC cover £10.99*

THE MOUNTAINS OF TURKEY *Karl Smith* Over 100 treks and scrambles with detailed route descriptions of all the popular peaks. Includes Ararat. *ISBN 1 85284 161 3 184pp PVC cover £14.99*

TREKS AND CLIMBS in WADI RUM, JORDAN *Tony Howard.* The world's foremost desert climbing and trekking venue. Masses of fantastic climbing.
ISBN 1 85284 254 7 252pp A5 Card cover £17.00

THE ALA DAG, Climbs and Treks in Turkey's Crimson Mountains *O.B.Tüzel* The best mountaineering area in Turkey. Destined to be one of the in-places. *ISBN 1 85284 112 5 296pp PVC cover £14.99*

TREKKING IN THE CAUCAUSUS *Yuri Kolomiets & Aleksey Solovyev* The great mountains hidden until recently behind the Iron Curtain. 62 walks of which half demand basic climbing skills. Included are the walks to the highest tops in Europe, the summits of Mt Elbrus. *ISBN 1 85284 129 X 224pp PVC cover £14.99*

ROCK CLIMBING IN HONG KONG *Brian J.Heard*
Great climbing for both locals and travellers. *ISBN 1 85284 167 2 136pp A5 size £12.99*

TECHNIQUES

ROPE TECHNIQUES *Bill March* Best selling handbook for experienced climbers, includes self-rescue techniques. *ISBN 1 85284 120 6 200pp £5.99*

SNOW & ICE TECHNIQUES *Bill March* Essential reading for all ice climbers. Emphasis on self-arrest. A best seller for many years. Updated by Bill Birkett. *ISBN 1 85284 238 5 96pp £5.99*

THE HILLWALKERS MANUAL *Bill Birkett* Everything the hillwalker needs to know from safety to photography. *ISBN 1 85284 111 7 152pp £7.99*

THE TREKKER'S HANDBOOK *Thomas R. Gilchrist* Everything a trekker needs to know, from gear to health. *ISBN 1 85284 205 9 A5 A5 size £10.99*

Send for complete Price List of over 280 books - walking, trekking, climbing etc.

Available from all good outdoor shops, bookshops or direct (include P&P) from **Cicerone Press, 2 Police Square, Milnthorpe, Cumbria LA7 7PY. Tel: 015395 62069**

PRINTED BY
CARNMOR PRINT & DESIGN, 95-97 LONDON ROAD, PRESTON,
LANCASHIRE, ENGLAND